LIFE IN THE
ORPHANAGE

Dave Foster

ISBN 0-9644613-1-5
Published by Top Tenn Press, Inc.
(423)249-1548 or (407)422-0455
E-Mail: TopTennPr@aol.com
Printed in the United States of America

0 1 2 3 4 5 6 7 8 9

This book is dedicated to anyone who has lived in an orphanage or who has traveled through childhood without the guidance and care of a loving parent.

Dave Foster

Edited by: Ida Percoco

Chapter Contents

Prologue

During the Fall of 1989, when my son Tim and I were on a short auto trip, I recalled a humorous event from my boyhood. He chuckled and then added,

"Dad, why haven't you told me more about the time when you were a kid?"

"That was long before you were born and I didn't think you'd be interested."

"Well, I've often wondered why you seldom talked about your childhood."

I focused my thoughts on the matter during the short lull in the conversation that followed. Tim's remark had thrown open a door to the long ago, a part of my life I wished to forget. Pain always came with its recall.

As my thoughts returned to the present I began to sense that my silence may have robbed Tim of some vital facts — details that indirectly helped to fashion his nature. He and his older brother, J. D., were privy to only a few bare details of my childhood. My father's early death had stopped the flow of our family's folklore. I had given little thought to this aspect until Tim asked about my early days.

His broaching the matter caused me to wonder just how much my painful life of the 1930s and 40s had affected him and his brother. The depth of his concern convinced me that I needed to fill in the details. Since the unique childhood had shaped both my spirit and outlook on life, perhaps it had also, in some measure, touched my sons' lives.

Tim's keen interest in the stories stirred those feelings and images of many years ago. I had thought, when in my late teens, that sometime in the future I might write a book. A concern for Mother's feelings had kept the idea at rest. While she was alive, I had refused to dig into those troubled times, for I didn't want my words to provoke her pain. Now, a few months after she had passed away, there was no reason to delay. I decided to write about my life in the orphanage.

The basic story would start in 1932 with my father's death, the event that prompted our mother and her four children to move to an orphanage. My two sisters, brother and I were all less than six years old at the juncture — I was four.

I planned to thrash out the feelings that filled my head and to write about the events of my fifteen-year stay. The memoir would end in 1947 with my finishing high school and leaving the orphanage. I had three objects in mind: To recall the frame of mind of a boy trapped in a hopeless situation, to describe the culture of a mid-1900 orphanage and to recount the forces that helped shape my personal outlook.

Instead of posting the events in the strict order which they happened, I planned to cluster the accounts under a dozen broad topics. A better telling of the story required that I use a chapter for each of these main themes.

From the outset, the project required more of me than simply to put the words on paper; it demanded that I visit anew those awful hurts from so many years ago. I stayed the course though the first draft, even in the face of the pain.

By refusing to talk, or even think, about these bad feelings, I had placed a time bomb in my psyche. There it had rested for years. During the first draft it seemed as if the situation was about to explode. Thankfully, a welcomed healing force soon moved in to replace the bad feelings.

Wishing to spare the other people who lived at the orphanage, I mainly wrote about my sisters, brother and myself. To fill in a few hard facts and still cover the full story, I needed to use a few names.

Many of the former residents hold a positive, more cheerful, view of life at the Home. The last few years I lived there were in that spirit, but the stretch from the first to the sixth was horrible.

My siblings, June Dempsey, Barbara Johnson and Fred Foster, have earned my sincere thanks. They have given me comfort and aid during this project just as they did years ago when we bonded to each other to travel childhood's lonely road.

Words alone cannot fully describe how my visit to the distant past has brought such a priceless gift. I hope you will also find value in this effort.

Thanks, Dave Foster.

Chapter 1

Newcomers

Seven hours after leaving Knoxville with Grandpa in his model-A Ford, we arrived at Clarksville. We drove through town on highway 41W and crossed the Red River. Grandpa pointed to a small embankment on his side of the road as we rounded the last corner of the trip, saying,

"That's a familiar sign; this must be the place."

Three giant links of chain formed by whitewashed stones sparkled on the bright green lawn near a large brick building. Centered in the links were the letters F, L and T, the emblem of Odd Fellowship. They stood for *Friendship Love and Truth*.

Beyond the first building were two more red brick structures. A stand of maple and white oak trees shaded the well-kept lawn. Whitewashed evenly up to 4 feet above the ground, the trees offered relief from the hot September day and gave the setting a look of distinction.

Grandpa stopped the car in front of the second, and main, building. Honeysuckle vines on a fence give off a sweet fragrance. Our long journey in the heat had ended at last. My grandfather, mother, two sisters, baby brother and I stepped out of the car and stretched to ease our stiff joints and muscles. We bunched together and trailed Grandpa to the sidewalk that led to the main building.

The front door opened and a man and woman appeared as we stepped on the sidewalk. He was about 40 years old, stocky but not fat. She was tall and thin. Grandpa abruptly stopped in his tracks. We all paused between the green metal benches that faced each other from opposite sides of the walk.

Grandpa was acting strange. Instead of walking, he stood as if frozen on the spot and gripped with both hands the lapels of his jacket.

"What's the matter with him?" I wondered! He didn't move a muscle, but fixed his eyes on the couple who walked toward us.

When they arrived, Grandpa smiled, moved from his statue-like stance and took the man's outstretched right hand. They shook vigorously.

"Brother Acree? I'm J. M. Dance, and this is my daughter Sophia Foster and her children."

The strange spell remained after the smiles and introductions. The four adults and four children stood for several moments as if wondering what would come next. Superintendent and Mrs. Grey Acree somehow seemed to intimidate Grandpa and Mother during this, their first meeting.

Fred, my eighteen-month old brother, tugged on Mother's dress to break the spell. She lifted him into her arms and we gathered around her. The oldest child, June, was not yet six. Barbara was two-and-a-half, and I was four.

After supper that first night, Mother tucked us in bed for what would prove to be the last time. She would sleep upstairs along with the cook and girls' matrons. All the children under six years of age stayed in the nursery supervised by Mrs. Acree. Grandpa left Clarksville the next morning and returned to his farm home near Knoxville, never again to visit the orphanage.

Something about this first meeting bothered me. I still cannot pinpoint the cause of my concern. Perhaps it was the stiff body language, the look on my mother's face, or simply that our lives had taken a bad turn with this change of address. This uneasy frame of mind and the few other details are the only things I recall about our arrival. Perhaps this was an omen of things to follow.

I would spend the next fifteen years in the Odd Fellows Home. A few of my experiences there were pleasant toward the end, but during the first ten years they ranged from just bearable to sheer hell. I felt trapped, knowing that I could not escape the orphanage. It was not a home — it was my prison.

Recalling those early years, I can feel again the despair, the pain of the penalties and the strain of the work load. It all began with our father's death in 1932, and our mother's decision to make the Odd Fellows Home a refuge for herself and four children.

We'll start with a brief family history. My father, Frederick Franklin Foster was born is 1899. Only a few sketchy tidbits of hearsay remain about his early life. His mother said that they adopted him. The story goes that a baby of Joe and Mattie Foster died in an accident involving runaway horses. They wanted to replace the child and found my father at the County Children's Home in Asheville, North Carolina. Mother had doubts about the account, for it had come from her mother-in-law with whom she did not get along.

A search of the Buncombe County official records yielded little. North Carolina started keeping birth records in 1906, several years after my father's birth. A later fire destroyed the court house at Asheville, and with it, some vital files. Trying to learn more about my father, I looked through the old records of the defunct children's home. I found nothing concrete. My efforts opened many questions about his early years, but there were few answers.

Several months after their marriage in 1924, Mother and Father made a trip to Asheville, North Carolina. They visited his mother, to whom my father had continued to send money. Tensions flared between the two women and their tiff ended in a bitter clash over the money. Contact between the two ended. They met only one other time — at my father's funeral. Mother tried to learn more about her deceased husband, but Father's mother would tell her nothing. This conflict between the women ended the verbal folklore from that side of the family due to his early death.

Mother knew that he had attended Christ School, a private boarding high school at Arden, North Carolina. I found his records there. He graduated at age eighteen during the First World War and enlisted in the Navy where he served aboard the USS Kimberly. After the war he moved to Knoxville and worked for the Railway Express Association (REA).

He boxed in bouts sponsored by the Golden Gloves, a group that boosted the sport during the 1920's and 1930's. His early wins gave him a chance at the state finals in Memphis. His days of prize-fighting ended with a solid defeat, but he stayed active in the sport and promoted several bouts in Knoxville.

Blood poisoning, caused by a ruptured appendix, took his life at age 33. Although only four years old at the time, I can recall a few incidents about our lives together.

I know more about my mother's background. Sophia Dance Foster, was the first of her immediate family to finish high school, graduating from Knoxville Young High in 1921. The following year, she took a teacher's course at the University of Tennessee.

The Knox County Superintendent of Schools offered her a teaching job at New Hopewell School near her home. Students in only the first and second grades attended the one room school. Although two boys as tall as Mother had attended for six years, they had remained in the second grade. Her teaching career ended after only two terms, for she was not able to control the boys. The next summer, she met my father at a picnic and married him a few months later.

My mother's mother, Laura Tipton Dance, told me how one of our ancestors came to these shores. Her mother's maiden name was Dixon. It seems that her ancestor and his brother often played near the docks in an Irish seaport where they lived. One day, some sailors struck up a conversation with the boys and offered to buy them a drink. Unaccustomed to the alcohol, the young boys soon fell into a stupor.

Upon awaking the next morning, the brothers saw that they were aboard a ship on the high seas. They had joined the crew the previous night, sailed with the tide and were heading to America. There was no turning back. The life of a seafarer did not appeal to either boy, so at the first port of call they managed to jump ship. The youths fled the coast and joined the Continental Revolutionary Army.

Granny's grandfather, the son of the unlikely sailor, moved to Tennessee in 1811. Although Granny Dance attended school only through the third grade, a measure of common sense always guided her actions. Many rural neighbors brought their problems, legal and otherwise, to her because she gave them gems of good advice. Her paternal forefather, Col. John Tipton, served in the legislatures of three different states and helped write Tennessee's first constitution.

Grandpa, as a young man, lived in a rural area known as The Fork of The Rivers, where the French Broad and Holston Rivers converge. He told how his father, during the Civil War, had organized a group of men to support the Union. They traveled to Kentucky and joined the U. S. Army.

My mother's parents married in 1896, bought a small mercantile store and settled in West Knoxville. In 1910, with five children to bring up, they felt the neighborhood had become an unfit place to live.

With the proceeds from the store they bought a farm, 117 hilly acres, in south Knox County. Although the rocky soil was fertile, it required hard work to make the land pay off. Besides eggs and butter, my grandparents produced both flowers and vegetables. On many days, they hauled their products to the Knoxville market. He rambled from stall to stall on Market Street, visiting with the other farmers, while she sold the bunches of irises, lilies or tulips.

James Marshall Dance joined the Independent Order of Odd Fellows (I.O.O.F.) in 1902. A Sunday School teacher and a cheerful man, Grandpa loved to tell a joke or good story. One, he loved to tell over and over.

"When I was a young man," Grandpa said, "a gentleman on horseback stopped at my father's place one day. He was looking for a James Marshall, and said a neighbor had told him where I lived.

"Seeing me, the man asked, 'Are you James Marshall?'

"'Yes sir, I am.'

"'Did you say I had a dance at my house last Saturday night?'

"'Yes sir, I did,' I confessed.

"When the man heard me admit to the deed, his eyes lit up with anger. He jumped off his horse with the intention of giving me a sound beating for spreading the wicked rumor.

"'My name is James Marshall DANCE,' I quickly added, 'I was at your house Saturday night.'"

Each time our grandfather told us this story he roared with laughter. He loved to entertain Fred and me, as he told us these yarns during the few occasions we were together after we left the orphanage.

Grandpa pointed to a steep slope from his front porch and said, "I plant potatoes on that hill because they're so easy to harvest. Once they're ripe, all I need do is dig the vine at the bottom. The rest of the potatoes just roll down into my sack." He enjoyed a good laugh.

Grandpa spent his last months as a patient at Eastern State Hospital. He suffered from the curse of the disease now known as Alzheimer's. In the early 1950s, we knew the illness as senility or hardening of the arteries. The ailment robbed him of his mental capacity near the end, but Grandpa never lost his perky sense of humor. He enjoyed good health on the day he drove us to the orphanage, eighteen years before his death.

After my father's death in 1932, Grandpa advised Mother to move to the orphanage with her four children. Several factors, one of which had to do with our country's near social and economic breakdown at the time, influenced her decision.

Most people those days lived with hardship knocking at their doors. The Great Depression had thrown its pall over the country. Many people were unable to find work and suffered from the same problems that helped to fuel a need for the orphanage.

The social safety nets of today did not exist in the early thirties. The engine that drove the country's business sputtered and failed; meanwhile the new relief programs came into being. The Social Security system paid its first benefits five years after we arrived at the orphanage. Aid to Dependent Children and Food Stamps were unknown. These and other public actions changed the social fabric of our country, but came years after our family needed them.

If a family joined the Odd Fellows or a similar group for protection, it gained a measure of security. This was a form of insurance, and many families looked to the Odd Fellows, swelling the role of such groups.

My father had followed my grandfather's lead and joined the Odd Fellows. They both played active roles in the local Neuberts Lodge. This qualified our family for help when the need came.

Our father, only thirty-three years old at his death, had earned a good income as head clerk at the Railway Express office. Tough problems faced the family when he died. The Odd Fellow order stepped in with a helping hand. One of the main reasons for their existence was to provide for their widows, orphans and aged members in need.

To this end, the Grand Lodge of Tennessee organized a home at a rural site near Clarksville. The local lodge had already started a dwelling for its aged and distressed members. In 1899, the other lodges joined to expand the facility, and the orphanage began to accept people from throughout the state.

Mother had very little work experience when our father died. Women seldom held industrial jobs during those days, a fact that would not change until several years later with the start of World

War II. Mother accepted the help offered and moved to the Clarksville orphanage with her four children.

June, Barbara, Mother, Fred and Author

Two other widows of Odd Fellows lived there with their off-spring. With a few exceptions, most of the Home's children were only half-orphans, as many still had one living parent. Over one hundred people lived at the orphanage in 1932, and its numbers were on the increase.

We joined the throng of other children, who ranged between three and eighteen years of age. Most children lived at the orphanage until they finished high school. The aged members, whether couples, widows or widowers, looked upon the Home as their refuge until the final days.

When we arrived, Fred was the youngest resident, and remained so for several years. Of the dozen or so aged people, Mr. S. R. Lee was the oldest. He would reach the age of ninety before Father Time used the reaper on him.

A Board of Trustees set the Home's general policy, but Mr. Grey Acree made the day to day decisions. At forty years old, and standing some five feet and eight inches tall, he looked a bit portly without being fat. He had held the job four years before we arrived, and would retire ten years later.

He assigned our mother the job of helping to manage the older girls. June, Barbara, Fred and I, all being under six years old, went to the nursery as was the custom. Mother's duties kept her away from the nursery, although she had asked that we live together as a family. To agree to such a request would upset the orphanage's routine.

Sorely missing the nightly routine of Mother's tucking me in, I sobbed myself to sleep several nights in a row. I can recall only a few details about Mrs. Acree's nursery other than the lonely nights caused by Mother's void. The wooden bench-boxes under the windows served as seats as well as for storing the few toys.

Mr. Acree's rule quickly led to trouble for Mother. She took a strong stand against breaking up the family. Fifty years after the fact, she outlined to me her fuss with him. Mother tried to keep the family intact, insisting that she be allowed to attend the needs of her children. He refused to back down and denied the request for a change in the rule. Mother rebelled.

This first standoff set the stage for added conflicts between the two. Mr. Acree viewed Mother's efforts as a threat to his routine and refused to grant a single request, whatever its nature. Their clashes came more often, and the relationship stretched to the breaking point. Wielding power from the high ground of superintendent, his word was final. These clashes, failing to end at the adult level, spilled over to include the four children.

After a few weeks, Mother decided that she could not live by the harsh rules. She found a clerking job and took an apartment in nearby Clarksville. From there she came to visit us often, but Mr. Acree soon claimed that her visits were upsetting the routine. Faced with the icy glares each time she came, she decided to leave Clarksville and return to Knoxville. There, she entered the Fort Sanders Hospital School of Nursing.

Knoxville is more than two hundred miles east of Clarksville. In the 1930's, the Greyhound bus covered this distance in seven hours. We saw less and less of Mother due to the travel problems and nursing school.

Her fewer and fewer visits left us with a great emptiness. We failed to understand her long absences, and this led to some deep emotional distress. Over time, our wounds grew deeper. Each child reacted to her absence according to his or her age at the time, with the youngest taking it the hardest.

By taking the futile stand with the boss, Mother had opened a state of conflict not only between herself and him but also between him and the children left behind. After she moved away, Mr. Acree still vented his wrath on us at the least provocation. Without mother, a feeling of deep despair cast a spell over my merge into the system.

> The lonely times demanded that my brother, sisters and I look to each other for emotional support.

June, Barbara, Fred and I still had each other. The lonely times demanded that my brother, sisters and I look to each other for emotional support. The strong glue of kinship sealed us into a tight family compact, prompting us to form a bond similar to those between identical twins. This unspoken union eased the pain and at the same time allowed us to endure the grief of our loss. Given the hurt of those early days, this strong tie gave me a bedrock of hope for the future. We remained a family of four in the midst of many other children.

Even though our compact was most helpful, it often brought me a great deal of anxiety. One of these times had to do with Barbara's possible adoption away from the Home. One day in the mid 1930s, I heard a visitor say to her,

"What's your name little girl?"

"Barbara Lee."

"Well, Barbara Lee, how would you like to come live with us?"

I grieved in silence, thinking that we were about to suffer the loss of Barbara. It's easy to see how this talk would start a rumor. She was a cute and bright child, but the visitor did not intend to adopt her. I didn't know that the Grand Lodge's policy precluded the adoption of children. My moods swung back and forth from anguish at losing Barbara to delight that she was about to escape our sad state. I relaxed only after I saw that the visitor's words were nothing more than idle talk.

Another crisis came when a bout with pneumonia put Fred to bed. He had endured the illness twice before but now, at age seven it had struck again. Jack Warren, a teenager and good friend to all the boys, had died of the disease about a year earlier. A rumor made the rounds that if a person came down with pneumonia for the third time he would surely die. My little brother was fighting this killer for the third time. Fred slowly regained his health after a week passed. Only then did I stop worrying.

When I was twelve years old, the pressures from my peers clashed with this family bond. To the exclusion of all others, most preteen boys wish to hang out with their own kind. They will not tolerate the younger boys who try to tag along. Those fresh pups just don't understand the world of the nearly grown boys. One instinctively subscribes to this bit of wisdom when he enters this phase of life. Its effects, nonetheless, gave me some bad moments.

A conflict between these points of view peaked one Sunday afternoon as we started our usual hike. In the view of my pals, the fact that Fred was three years younger, made him an outsider. Although we had not invited them to come along, Fred and two smaller boys followed us into the woods. Sensing this problem, we older boys solved it with our feet. We ran hard until the boys who followed fell behind, but that's when the tactic began to trouble me.

Even after the other two had turned back, Fred still tried to keep up with the older boys. Chasing along behind us, now alone, he yelled to me,

"Wait for me Buddy, Bud-deee wait for me."

Although his pleading voice retreated into the distant woods behind us, it tugged at my feelings. Should I keep running with my peers or should I stop and wait for my little brother? If I answered his call, my friends would pepper me with ridicule and snide remarks. The peer pressure won out. I kept running, but Fred's forlorn cries still rang in my mind even after he was out of my hearing range.

This family bond offered me something to hold to during the early days. Without it, life in the Home would have been much harder to take. Except for a few details, the events from the early thirties remain a bit murky. I can recall a few problems we had fitting into the institution's life. The rules separated us according to age and gender. Stern and exact customs, including a new routine of formal dining, required that we adjust to a strange way of doing things. We quickly had to master a set of "does and don'ts" that the boss strictly enforced.

The ideal life of our Knoxville home had ended, but the memory of it still lingered. Comparing the earlier times to this new lifestyle at the orphanage, I sensed the profound changes. The contrast was severe, and I sorely missed the love and security of our former home.

Years later, and a short time after Mother's death, I again felt the depth of this blissful love that had filled our Knoxville home. I was going through her things when a yellowed paper fell from the pages of her high school yearbook. I carefully unfolded the sheet to find a poem drafted in her hand. In the exact form that she penciled it, Mother's verse reads:

A HAPPY HOME

We have a boy and we have a girl,
Our home is completely blessed,
And we are surely serenely happy
As four little birds in their nest.

No matter how long we may live,
Our hearts and minds cannot be
As gracious and thankful enough
To our Heavenly Father, you see.

One is named David, the other one June.
Oh! They are a perfect pair.
We hope and pray we can rear them sweet
And innocent, and perfect and fair.

With our dear Heavenly Father's help,
(And without it, a failure we'd be)
We can train and guide our little ones Dear
To be just as good as good can be.

Since she named June and me, but not Barbara and Fred, Mother must have written the lines a few years before Father's death. This dates the poem between mid 1928 and late 1929. Until

Father's death in 1932 we lived a happy lifestyle in sharp contrast to our new setup — four grieving children in a strange place far removed from the joy-filled home and loving parents.

A few months after our arrival at the orphanage, June turned six and moved to the dorm for young girls. My move from the nursery came almost too late, that is, not before I had suffered a few bad moments. One day Mrs. Acree gave Fred and me a bath in the same tub. I began to squirm, trying to cover my nakedness. Soon thereafter, some two years after we arrived, the boss moved me out of the nursery to the boys' building. Fred and Barbara remained.

Among all those bad times of our early days, I recall one pleasant detail. Fred, as the youngest child, became a hit with the older girls. They vied for a chance to hold, cuddle, and care for him. The old folks also showed a special interest in the boys and girls; they doted over the small ones and played the role of surrogate grandparents. It seemed that everyone favored my little brother, but I'm getting ahead of the story.

In a strange way, an accident has helped me recall events from my early life. One day when I was ten years old, we were breaking-in a team of new oxen. We had yoked them before, but had now hitched them to a wagon for the first time. I tried to keep the animals calm by walking backward in front of them when my foot caught on a rock. I stumbled and plunged to the ground. This sudden move excited the thousand pound oxen and they bolted. An intense fear gripped me as I fell — the pounding hooves or wagon wheels were about to crush me.

This terror brought a flow of events rushing through my mind. One by one they zipped by to cover my entire life. A parade of "this is your life" topics began with my earliest memory and ended at the then current accident. As the scenes whizzed by, I was able to discern each incident. The most vivid scenes were those surrounded by an element of stress or anxiety.

I was not able to change the events as they flashed by. Strangely, I could stop and examine any scene at will, freezing the moment and viewing the event as if were an instant replay on television. I searched for an answer to my current plight. The entire review ended before I hit the ground.

Without trying to explain further, I suppose the state of panic brought on this scroll of incidents. Good fortune allowed me to come through without a scratch. The wagon ran over me but I somehow missed the wheels. The accident brought to view a few scenes that I could not have otherwise recalled. These dated from my early days in Knoxville.

The first involved the celebration of my third birthday. Mother made a big issue of giving me the choice to select the type of cake. I swelled with a feeling of self-worth as I chose a white cake with white icing. Similar emotions came with my recall of the times my father took me with him when he exercised. I sat in the high school bleachers alone and watched him jog around the track.

In one scene we arrived home from Sunday School and pulled into our driveway. June spied a friend and asked Father to stop the car and let her out. He agreed. I also jumped out the opposite side. As the car moved forward my foot landed under the rear wheel. Until I screamed, Father thought that I was still in the back seat. The injury was not serious, but I felt that Father had willfully run over me. Years later, Mother confirmed the incident, and that she knew of my thoughts.

The next item, coming to mind due to my problem with the oxen, concerned a report that a mad dog roamed loose near our Knoxville home. June, Barbara, and I pressed our noses to the screen door, attempting to catch sight of the canine. Fred was too young to walk. I already knew about mad dogs. Talk of them filled me with fright. Mother put her arms around me and convinced me that we were safe, that no dog could come through the latched screen door. Her concern and words of assurance, in the face of danger, changed my panic feelings to poise.

Next, when I was almost four years old, a strong curiosity tempted me to make a solo trip around the block. All went well until a neighbor boy approached me. When I entered the alley behind our house, he asked in a tone of voice that made me wish I had never left home,

"Where do you think you are going, boy?"

"Nowhere,"

My heart beat like a drum, and I could barely talk.

He grabbed my arm and pulled me into his darkened basement. I began to cry. His mother heard my screams and came to investigate. She told him to release me, and I ran home.

Mother had already started looking for me. Her voice rang with anger.

"Next time, ask for permission before you decide to leave this house alone."

She loosely tied me to the bedstead, but in my mind, the scare in the neighbor's basement had been enough punishment. Sobbing and protesting the discipline, I remained tied up for about 30 minutes. This flash-by event prompted a mix of emotions, ranging from fear to that of double jeopardy before she set me free.

A scene from my fourth year flashed by. Mother dressed me in a new suit, shirt and tie. I swelled with pride — this was the first time I wore long pants.

"You look like a little gentleman."

"Wow!" I thought, "In Mother's eyes I'm a little man." With this voice of confidence, my sense of self-worth reached a new height. I saw myself as a grownup. These good feelings of the flashback carried over into the next day.

I wore my new suit to church. A group of somber people stood near the rear door. Sobbing broke the silence as we walked down the aisle. A big surprise awaited me when we reached our front-row seats. There lay my father in an opened casket covered by a piece of sheer white lace. "What is Daddy doing there, I wondered?"

He appeared to be asleep. I had not been told he was dead.

At home after the funeral, and after she regained her composure, Mother hugged me and said,

"David, your father has gone to be with Jesus, and since you're the older son, you are now head of the family."

I sensed that my first duty was to help Mother dry her tears.

"Don't cry Mom. Everything will be okay," I assured her.

From that moment, Mother stopped talking down to me, as a parent speaking to a child, but started using an adult tone of voice. This job as head of the family, or simply the thought behind it, placed a heavy load on my shoulders. Viewed through the eyes of a child, I accepted the idea, if not the fact, of the extra load.

This series of thoughts from long ago, even now, zooms in to spark anew a burning agony. I keep the doors to this room of my memory closed. By refusing to think about the events, I have built a fire wall. It protects me from the flames and heat of the pain.

When I review all these events, a few questions arise in my adult mind. During those first days of her widowhood, what thoughts about the children's future passed through my mother's head? How did she endure those days at the Odd Fellows Home? How did she handle the emotional onslaught caused by Mr. Acree's rulings? Given the nature of their clashes, did a normal maternal instinct prompt her judgment to leave us at the orphanage? Did Mother do what was best for her young, or was she relieved that she no longer had to provide for us?

Until her dying days, some sixty years later, Mother nurtured the ill will she felt toward Mr. Acree. I tried to project myself into her place. What drove her decisions? Was there a bit of wisdom in her acts? Did she take a careful look at all the choices open to her, or did she miss some viable options?

In the early 1930's, women had few chances to work outside the home. Surely, the hard times influenced her. She and her four children needed all the basics — food, clothing, shelter, and nurture.

I discussed these matters with Mother many years after the fact, but I still cannot put the main question to rest. Was it necessary for her to leave four children in the orphanage for fifteen years? The question begs a response, but the answer refuses to come. Now, with the benefit of hindsight, I question: Did Mother make the correct decision?

Her parent's farm was large enough to serve the needs of our extended family in 1932. The grown children no longer lived at home. My grandfather died before we build a real bond, but I had a number of talks with my grandmother years after leaving the orphanage. She was a loving and good-hearted person. Had Granny known about our problems at the orphanage, she would have pulled us to her bosom with open arms. That is, if Mother had sought her help.

Mother had an awesome task -- to provide for the well-being of teh family. Her big problem, the burden of earning a living for five people, came during the Great Depression. This convinced her that the orphanage was the best place for four small children. Her late husband belonged to the Odd Fellows. The order's main credo was to offer aid to members caught in a circumstance such as the one we faced. After all, shouldn't she accept the ready-made solution to the crisis?

June, Fred, Barbara and Author

Should Mother have remained nearby, once she decided that we children were to live at the orphanage without her? Even with the bad relationship with Mr. Acree, did she choose the best option? True, she needed to learn a trade, but there were other things to consider. How could she have foreseen the true pattern of our life at the orphanage? Unless there was good cause, why would any woman hand over her parental duties to a Mr. Acree? Faced with the set of facts, did her maternal instincts prescribe her reply or did other motives decide the issue? Did pride play a role?

Mother's answer to her problem with Mr. Acree changed our lives. As a small boy without a loving mother at my side, I felt forsaken. A motherless child in the situation would not have faced such torment, but my hurt and despair surfaced each time I thought about our mother. I had a mother, somewhere. This knowledge stirred the ill feelings I harbored. I eagerly looking forward to Mother's visits, and suffered when the spans between them grew longer and longer. The orphanage was a lonely place as one absence lasted for three years.

The comfort I drew from my sisters and brother made life bearable. This family unity of four children gave me purpose and strength to face the daily trials.

The bond endured. As the newest children we faced the problem of falling in line with the orphanage's rules. We soon learned that the slightest infraction, even a minor misdeed, brought certain and swift punishment.

I felt trapped, left to drown in a tide of bitter emotions, with little help to rescue me from the despair. This early period at the orphanage hurt the most. I nursed the constant agony. The mental anguish of those years demanded that I ignore the past and focus on the future. I became restless; I wanted to grow up fast, but seemingly the time passed ever so slowly.

Through the years, I eagerly looked for tomorrow; a new day would bring better times. My life struck bottom when we went to the orphanage, and it could only move up. Forever looking to pull myself from the quagmire, I sensed that life did improve bit by bit over time.

For fifteen years I looked forward to the day of my departure. I loathed being stuck at the orphanage, an idea that filled my thoughts until reaching the mid-teen years. The notion softened as I moved into the late teens, but only after a childhood that crawled ever so slowly. Upon starting high school, I took a more upbeat view of my status. The former loathing turned into hope. Each passing year seemed to bring a mark of progress. Sensing this gain, I came to believe that the passage of time and betterment were the same thing.

In the Spring of 1947, I had spent over 75 percent of my life at the orphanage. The special moment I'd anticipated so long arrived at last and the dark interlude ended. On that brilliant day in May, I rounded the corner on a one-way trip and refused to look back.

Chapter 2

Facilities

A huge sign mounted on the central, and largest of three red brick buildings, carried the words ODD FELLOWS HOME. The many trees, whitewashed to four feet above ground, added sparkle to the beautifully kept grounds. Other buildings sat on both sides of the main structure. Concrete sidewalks linked the three. All of this formed a pleasant scene.

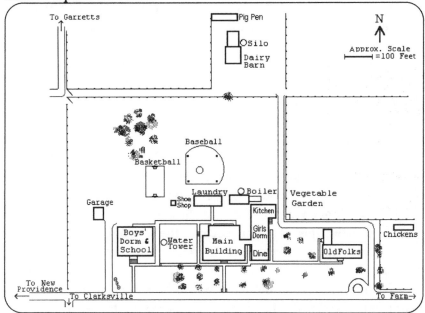

Physical Layout of the Main Facilities

The residential buildings, barns and cemetery spread across some 35 acres. This left about 125 acres, out of the total 260, for farming. Only a hundred-acre tract remained undeveloped. We knew this plot as Garretts. Its hilly pristine land lay a mile north-west of the main building. From time to time, we sharecropped a few acres owned by neighbors.

The amenities of the Home ranked it, during the early 1930's, as an ultra modern dwelling. All the lived-in buildings had running hot and cold water, indoor toilets and electric lights. A furnace supplied steam for central heating.

The Independent Order of Odd Fellows built and supported this home for both their orphans and needy aged members. The I.O.O.F. is a fraternal order that subscribes to a set of noble virtues. Non-sectarian, the order's "Great Commands" require its members to: "Visit the Sick, Relieve the Distressed, Bury the Dead, and Educate the Orphan." The Odd Fellows' emblem, formed by three links of chain, stands for the motto that binds the members in "Friendship, Love, and Truth."

Communication is one of the order's main goals. The members instruct, advance, and exalt through a set of rituals and degrees. In one sense, the Brotherhood works much like a mutual insurance firm. The members help each other by paying annual dues and following the "Great Commands." It's a group effort.

The order arrived in America during the early 1800's. The first lodge on this side of the Atlantic began on March 27, 1819. Mr. Thomas Wildey was an active lodge member from England. He planted the first seed by advertising in the _Baltimore American_ and asking that Odd Fellows meet with him.

He, along with the few prospects who answered the ad, started a Baltimore branch. After The Manchester Unity of England issued them a charter, this new unit became the Washington Lodge. The order's records in Great Britain date from the early sixteenth century.

From its beginning the New World branch grew rapidly. Thirty years later, in 1850, the order had increased to nearly 175,000 members and over 2,000 lodges. By the year 1900, more than a million people had joined. Including the women's arm of the order known as Rebekahs, the network of lodges had increased to some 15,000 units.

The Odd Fellows continued its fast growth rate into the early years of the 20th century. My father joined a lodge in 1922, soon after he married. By that time, active lodges functioned in most large cities as well as many small towns throughout the country.

The Grand Lodge of Tennessee founded the Odd Fellows Home in 1898. By paying a fifty-cent head tax, the members throughout the state gave the Home its financial start. Member lodges and Odd Fellows sent clothes and other items of support. Many Rebekah groups also helped with added gifts.

The orphanage's farm started with very poor soil. By using good farming methods, the workers increased the crop harvest over time. Within a few years, the children grew most of the food they consumed. They harvested ample stocks of grain and vegetables, raised pigs and fowl, and produced milk.

Fifteen years after the Home's doors opened the residents numbered 124 people: one aged man, three widows, 58 boys and 62 girls. By the time our family arrived in 1932, nearly 200 people lived at the orphanage.

Main Building

The main building had served as a large private home before becoming an orphanage. Its front porch extended around the left side of the structure. Stocks of summer flowers lined the porch's wide railings. These plants, and their red clay pots and green wooden boxes, spent the winter months in a sun room directly above the porch. This brilliant facade of flowers behind the green lawn looked beautiful, but it took much work.

When I visualize this scene of the orphanage, other pictures come to mind and fill out my mental image. For example, Mrs. Acree supervised the young boys who carried the flower pots from the porch to the sun room each fall. The job took about half a day. During the biannual trek the next spring, we reversed the parade of flowers and moved nearly a hundred containers. Although I hated the task, I often found myself among the boys tapped to do it.

Besides these special jobs, Mr. Acree gave every boy and girl a daily chore. He monitored each task, making sure that the person assigned performed the work. My sister June's ongoing job was watering and caring for the flowers. Playing nursemaid to this battery of flowers became drudgery for her, and over fifty years would pass before she could stand to keep any blossoms around her home.

Once I reached the age of six, I moved from the nursery to the boys' building. Mr. Acree gave me the job of keeping part of the front lawn clear of tree limbs, debris and litter. Later, he made me responsible for the entire lawn. I scanned the lawn each morning, removed any trash I found and continued to check the area throughout the day.

This job, which I held for several years, gave me a high visibility. If my efforts failed to meet Mr. Acree's wishes, he punished me. This soon taught me that a clean lawn meant harmony and a dirty lawn spelled trouble. If I missed a toy, twig, or scrap of paper the superintendent's wrath came down hard. I soon learned to accept the charge of an assigned task. This helped me acquire a healthy will to work.

From the age of 10 years, I kept the grounds mowed — a chore that called for added muscle power. I cut the lawn with a push-type mower. Several patches of tough Bermuda grass made this hard work.

If the mower developed a problem I became a hands-on mechanic. The curved reel blade often slipped out of adjustment. I carried a screwdriver and a pair of pliers to keep the blade properly positioned, otherwise the blade tended to chew instead of to cut the grass. During one session of endless problems, I decided to fix the mower for good. The machine worked well after I took it apart and added jam nuts to the screws.

The main building housed the nursery, parlor and library as well as Mr. Acree's living quarters. The former nursery room served as our grade school for three years, ending with the 1941-42 term. On the upper floor of the building were the sun porch, a girls' reading room and rooms for the cook and matron.

The building's large basement extended below ground at the front, but a slope set it at ground level in the rear. Our plumbing shop occupied a long slender room nearby — one that I well remember.

An older boy, who served as the plumber, ruled the shop as if he owned the place. Whenever I, or any other small boy, walked in, he'd yell,

"What do you want in here, boy?"

"Nothing," I'd answer sheepishly.

"Then take nothing and get out."

As I turned to walk out, he'd say in a more friendly tone, "Now, what are you looking for?"

The girls ironed the freshly laundered clothes in a room next to the plumber's shop, and sorted dirty clothes in another. Beneath the front parlor and the superintendent's quarters was a crawl space, a spot that holds some special memories from the later years.

One day, as a high school student walking home from the bus stop, I spied an unusual object in the weeds near a phone pole. It was a piece of equipment that a lineman had lost or had thrown away. An ear piece clipped across the operator's head and a neck strap held the speaker on the chest. This allowed the free use of hands.

I always wanted to know how things worked, so I picked up the discarded phone. It seemed that a broken wire was its only problem. Would the thing work if I fixed the wire? Eager to test it, I'd have to wait for the opportune time — meaning, a time when the boss was away from his desk.

My chance came one day when the superintendent went to town. I entered the musty crawl space under his office. Using a flashlight, I searched for the phone line. I soon found the wires supported by ceramic insulators nailed to the floor joists. Through a hole in the floor, the wires led to the office phone above. I stripped the insulation from the two lines and attached my newly repaired phone.

"Number please," asked the female voice.

This standard response that the phone operators used those days brought a broad smile to my face.

I spit out a three-digit number and surprised my girlfriend with a phone call. In the days that followed, I phoned her at each opportune moment. One day after we had talk for several minutes, I heard footsteps above me. Someone walked into the superintendent's office. Two voices told me that June and a friend had come in to make a call. They too, had waited until they found the office vacant before placing a call.

June presented me with a problem when she took the ear piece from its hook. What should I do? Identify myself? No, I wanted to keep the private phone a secret.

"Number please," I said in a concealed voice.

She gave the number.

I answered in the same deep-tone voice, "Line's busy."

She cradled the ear piece and excitedly said to her friend,

"Did you hear that? The phone company has a man operator!"

I kept the phone my secret and used it over the next several months to place many calls from my own private office under the main office.

A two-story hallway linked the dining room and kitchen wing to the main building. Two dorms for girls occupied the second floor of this wing, with the older girls using the one at the rear. The dining hall, large enough to seat two hundred people, was on the wing's first floor. The girls entered the dining area from the hallway and the boys entered through an outside front door. Four large, square wooden columns supported a second floor room. This shielded the boys from the elements as they waited before entering to eat.

The dining hall, and kitchen behind it, sat above a large basement. We used one of the several lower rooms to process milk. A hand-cranked machine converted fresh milk into cream and skimmed milk, or 'blue John,' as we knew it. For years, the rusted-out equipment for making large blocks of ice sat idle in the next room — I cannot recall a time that it was in use.

A room directly below a huge refrigerator that stood against the rear wall of the dining room housed its cooling unit. This machine often spewed out strong fumes of ammonia. Nearby rooms contained a pantry of canned goods and large storage bins for potatoes.

One year as we harvested the sweet potato crop, Mr. Acree gave me a special task in this part of the basement, saying,

"Buddy we need to store the new crop in a warm and dry place, so I want you to build a fire in the stove and keep it going for the next few days. After we dig the first couple of bushels, I want you to place the yams into the storage bins one by one. Take care not to bruise them. The other boys will dig and bring the potatoes from the fields."

I loved the taste of sweet potatoes, so after the stove heated and before the second load arrived, I fixed myself a snack. I held the job as kitchen boy at the time, so I had access to the skillet and butter needed for cooking the fresh roots. After I had eaten one batch, and started the butter sizzling in the pan for the second, the boss walked in.

He used his belt to discipline me on the spot, but I had already enjoyed the first snack. A stomach nearly full of the tasty reward was worth the whipping.

Old Folks Building

"HOME FOR OUR AGED" read the large sign mounted on the upper porch of the L-shaped, red brick structure. This building stood at the highest point of the area, some two hundred feet east of the main building. Four large white columns supported a wooden upper porch that afforded a striking view toward the south beyond the Cumberland River. On the porch a set of outside stairs connected the full-width upper and lower levels. The old folks lived in rooms large enough to sleep three or four people each. This building had once served as the orphanage hospital.

The chicken house was a short distance further to the east. It was a wooden, 15 by 60 foot, tin-roofed structure. Besides the daily harvest of eggs, each spring we dined on tender fried chicken. We grew corn, ground it and fed it to the flock of hens. Working as kitchen boy after age ten, I gathered eggs each day and from time to time cleaned the chicken house.

The social activity of the flock fascinated me — I noted that the largest and strongest chickens hogged most of the food while the weakest often went without. The stronger ones formed a pecking order. The creatures ranked according to size and spirit, or the lack thereof. The strongest chickens plucked the feathers off those in the lowest caste. These sad creatures suffered badly, and often ended up totally stripped of their plumage. I wondered if humans ever copied these tactics.

The small children used a playground located between the main and old folks' building. From their quarters, the aged residents could sit and watch the young people at play. In front of the building, near a turn-around circle in the road, was a small merry-go-round. Although muscle power turned it, we spent hour upon hour riding the machine. As small children we also enjoyed the seesaws, a sand box and a tall but sturdy swing set.

Three swings hung from a twelve-foot high framework of iron pipes. We looked upon these as flying machines and spent many hours pumping. I often tried to fly fast enough to loop over the top, but could never swing that high.

Boys' Building and School

The boys lived in a brick structure built in 1912. It sat about one hundred feet west of the main building. The first floor, some six feet above the ground level, housed a two-room school and auditorium as well as the boss's office. Two dorms, a study room and the band master's quarters occupied the second floor. Besides a small basketball gym, the basement housed a shower room, a carpenter shop and an electric shop. Another basement room housed the boys' clothes.

Each Saturday afternoon, the boys gathered in the basement to swap their dirty clothes for a set of clean garments. Under Mr. Acree's policy we received a clean shirt, a pair of overalls and a cotton nightgown each week, but no underwear. We didn't use it. Since we spent the summer bare footed, we received socks only in the winter.

> Each Saturday afternoon, the boys gathered in the basement to swap their dirty clothes for a set of clean garments.

During the first seven years of my stay, this scheme remained in effect. Although the practice was a good way to distribute the clothes, I saw it as a big drawback. It did not allow for personal ownership.

A large open room extended the full width and breadth of the third floor. This gave us an excellent place to play during the cold or rainy weather. One event that involved the room sparks both good and bad memories. One summer our dog brought in a colony of fleas that infested the room. Whenever a person walked to the head of the stairs the insects sensed an approaching meal. These blood-thirsty pests were vicious, so we were willing to try anything to keep from becoming their target. We sprayed the room several times, but failed to rid the room of fleas.

Someone proposed a bizarre way to overcome fleas. This novel idea deserved a trial, as all the other attempts had failed. It involved our putting four sheep in the attic and leaving them there a couple of days. The fleas flocked to this new source of blood, but it didn't bother the sheep. The natural lanolin in their wool killed the fleas. This ended our problem, but what a mess. It took a big cleanup project before we regained the use of our playroom.

Rows of single beds lined the two dorms on the second floor. A four-inch thick mattress covered the flat springs of the iron beds. The boys who attended grade school slept in one room, while the high school aged boys used the other. Every morning, we folded our night gowns, placed them under the pillows and made our beds.

In spite of the dorm's tall ceilings, at times a hot and breezeless summer night made sleeping inside nearly impossible. During these spells, I often moved my sheets outside to the fire escape attached to the building. Under a black sky dotted by the brilliant light specks of the milky way, I could escape the heat but not the iron-hard bed. A melodious whippoorwill often lulled me asleep in the cool night air.

A common washroom served both boys' dorms. Each evening we brushed our teeth and washed our faces, hands, and feet in this room. Here, Mr. Acree, as did Mr. York who preceded him, held a nightly ritual. They checked for dirty feet and made sure that we brushed our teeth as we prepared for bed, but our worry level raised each night.

At this time, the boss punished any boy who needed the discipline. After charging the target boy with the bad deeds done during that day, he dispensed the penalty. Lifted the nightgown above the boy's bare buttocks, he lined it with red whelp marks.

The boy admitted his guilt and made a fruitless plea for clemency during the flogging. He yelled,

"I won't ever do it again, Mr. Acree, please stop. I'm sorry. I won't ever do it again."

Until the boss ended the whipping the boy cried and shouted. With the ordeal over, and when back in the dorm with the other boys, the target boy often made an effort to save face. Speaking in a macho tone that only those nearby could hear, he said with an air of confidence

"He didn't hurt me one bit."

Refuting the boy's fearless boast, the whelps argued a more proper and telling story. We always tied to evade Mr. Acree's belting, but that was nearly out of the question.

One evening after study hall, several of us boys milled around in the reading room on the second floor. We were listening to the radio. I was eleven. Don, who had a few years on me, pulled a knife from his pocket and said,

"I whetted my knife sharp as it can get."

"Here Buddy, hold this string, and I'll show you."

I took the string, and using both hands, pulled it tight in front of my chest. Don struck a slashing blow, but he completely missed the target. Instead, his knife opened a gash two inches long on the back of my left hand. Though the bleeding ended soon, we both dreaded how Mr. Acree would react to my sliced hand. We fabricated a tale to explain the wound.

Our story had it that I cut myself on a cracked glass while trying to open a stuck window. The scheme worked — the boss punished no one, but my hand still shows the scar.

I did not move into the older boys' dorm. When it was time for me to start high school, the census at the orphanage had lowered and we had moved out of the boys' quarters.

The building remained in use. Soon after we vacated, two dozen young men arrived by bus. They were the first rookie class Tennessee's mounted highway patrol. Our former abode was to serve both as their school and living complex.

Early in their training program, the men learned how to ride a motorcycle with a sidecar attached. We watched these events with great interest. During this stage, the trainees often allowed us to ride as they motored around the area. With siren shrieking at full blast we prized the thrill of a cruise in the sidecar.

A few months before the patrolmen arrived, Mrs. Kate McDaniel, one of our school teachers, died suddenly. Five teachers had worked in the Home's school when it bustled with its highest number of residents. The school moved to the main building in 1943, and by then, only one teacher remained. Even after this move, a few children who lived near the orphanage attended our school. The last teacher, Mrs. Frances Hambaugh, taught me through the sixth grade.

Late in 1942, the U. S. Army began to build Camp Campbell nearby. The many workers who flocked to the area soon caused a shortage of local housing. We cut the former boys' building into living quarters for renting to the new people. A bit later, the old folks also moved into the main building; this opened more rental units for the defense workers.

Other Buildings

Two smaller structures behind the boys' building included a garage for the school bus and a shoe-repair shop. A basketball court, with a clay surface, occupied a site a few yards behind the boys' building. Until razed in 1935, a wooden cottage that housed the old men stood at this spot.

A large, up-to-date steam laundry was behind the main building. Twice weekly, a team of girls and boys fired up the plant. Whether in the clammy heat of mid-summer or in the freezing cold of winter, the crew worked with a vigor seldom seen in other laundries. They loaded the dirty overalls, and other soiled garments, into two giant washers that tumbled the items clean. The wash then moved in canvas carts to a spin dryer.

After spinning, some of the damp goods moved on roller racks into a steam heated drying room. The moist sheets and other flat items went to a mangle for ironing. Two girls loaded the machine, and two other girls caught and folded the items that rolled out of this giant presser. The laundry boy pushed the large canvas carts of washed and dried clothing to the main building. In this chatter-filled, basement room a dozen girls sorted, hand pressed and folded.

In the later years we fired the laundry once a week, and then used only a portion of the building. The west end housed the bus after the renters started using the garage. We also set aside one corner for butchering hogs and curing the meat.

The first frosty-cold day of late fall meant that hog-killing time had arrived. One season stands out in my memory because of the double work it meant for Fred and me. I was seventeen. That year, we butchered seven hogs that weighed in at about three hundred pounds each. After trimming the hams, shoulders and slabs of bacon, we buried the meat in a salt box and left it there for several days. This was only the first part of the curing process. Afterward, when preparing to smoke the meat, we washed away the salt and gave the pieces a final trim.

Some meat did not go to the salt box. After cutting the fat trimmings into small cubes, we put them into a large black-iron kettle over a roaring wood fire. When cooked, these fragments rose to the top and floated like little boats in a sea of hot lard. We seined these chunks, now called cracklings, from the grease and saved them for adding to cornbread mix. We poured the lard into five-gallon cans and used it for general cooking.

Some of the lard we converted into soap. We filled a V-trough with ashes from the fire, poured water on, and allowed it to soak through. We then caught the liquid that drained from the ashes and mixed it with the hot grease. Presto, it congealed into brown lye soap.

The other parts of trimmed meat, besides those cut from the hams and shoulders, became sausage. We seasoned the pork with salt and hot peppers, and using a hand-cranked machine, ground these chunks. We then stuffed the meat into casings that the girls had sewed from cotton cloth. The three-feet-long bags were three inches in diameter. With this work complete, we were ready to hang and smoke the other cuts of pork along with the sausage.

Before hanging the meat, we built a framework needed to support the load, for this was the first time we used the laundry as a smoke house. The frame extended from one corner of the building. Y-shaped posts supported two fifteen-feet-long beams at one end, and brackets attached to the wall held the other ends.

First, we tied the hams, shoulders and slabs of bacon to six-foot long sticks. The jowls and sausage sacks went on other poles. Placing the heavy loads of meat took much energy, so both Fred and I eagerly looked forward to finishing the job plus a well-earned rest.

Fred said, "Here's the last load of hog jowls."

"Crack."

The loud sound echoed through the building when I placed that final load on the beam.

I yelled "Look out."

The massive weight had split one of the Y-post supports and the entire seven-hog batch of pork crashed to the concrete floor. Fred stood under the meat when the framework gave way, jumping just in time to save himself from injury. From my place on the ladder, I watched in utter disbelief. What a mess!

Although uninjured, we could not escape the extra work. We washed the meat, repaired the framework and again hung the pork. The smoking process was ready to begin. Using green hickory wood for flavor and sawdust to encourage smoke, we built small fires under the meat. The fire burned for several days. Because the laundry building was so big, it did not make a good smoke house.

A brick building only a few feet east of the laundry housed the coal-fired boiler. It supplied steam heat and hot water to the laundry and other buildings.

During the later years, the job of minding the boiler fell to me. Each morning I stoked the boiler's flames alive and fed coal to the monster based on the need for steam and hot water. That evening I banked the fire box. An overheated boiler running low on water can explode, so the steam pressure and water gauges were always in my thoughts. This work would last for only a few months before we closed down the furnace.

At times, the girls opened a window in their dorm that towered above the boiler to demand hot water. They shouted in unison,

"Make the hot water hotter, please."

This meant that I needed to shovel more coal into the furnace.

A low area large enough to serve as our baseball diamond was north of the furnace and laundry. After each rain the field turned into a muddy sump, forcing us to wait several days for it to dry before we played ball. Many tons of the red clay needed to make bricks for the main buildings had come from the site.

The dairy barn and silo sat beyond the baseball diamond, some 200 yards north of the main building. During a baseball game one Sunday afternoon, a spectator with the visiting team shouted,

"Knock it over the church house."

A confused fan saw the cupola on top of the dairy barn and thought it sat on the top of a church building. Our crowd roared with laughter at the blooper, but the incident gave the orphanage team a lasting battle cry. "Knock it over the church house" often rang out as our player stepped up to bat.

Two other barns were a quarter mile east of the main building. Closer to the crop fields, the largest of these housed the farm tools, work animals and feed. We cured tobacco in the other.

Garretts

Years before we arrived, the orphanage had bought a tract of land from people active in the tobacco trade. Garretts, as we knew the hundred-acre parcel, lay a mile north of the main building. We used the land to graze cattle and to supply drinking water, but in other ways it remained a pristine wonderland. A beautiful stream flowed past three hills studded with trees. The magic of Garretts offered a refuge and supplied untold thrills to the boys. I logged many hours of fun and frolic there while making water wheels, engaging in war-game sports and hunting for poison snakes.

One day, we decided to build a swimming hole, and moved tons of dirt to erect a dam across the creek. The rains came a few days later and raised the lake enough for us to swim. Soon a summer cloudburst caused a swift current to wash out the spillway. This destroyed our new dam.

Many species of trees grew at Garretts; among them oak, maple and poplar. We gathered black walnuts, hickory nuts and chestnuts without adult direction. Our stained fingers gave witness to the walnut harvest each fall. We ate some nuts, and sold some as well, but a blight killed all the chestnut trees in 1945.

A plant called May apple grew beneath the trees at Garretts. I don't know why the roots of these 10-inch-tall plants were valuable, but we dug and sold them to a Clarksville scrap dealer. Perhaps the drug firms used the plants to make medicine.

We also dug sassafras roots, collected water cress and gathered mint. Our efforts along this line brought little more than pennies, but since we had so little money, the harvest was a super cash crop. We traded the cash for candy bars.

Many blackberry vines grew on the hills and in the dells of Garretts. Our role changed with this crop; Mr. Acree took charge of the picking and required that the berries be used to make jam or jelly. A group of boys and girls went to Garretts several days during the July berry-picking season. Each person worked with a quota, that is, to pick one gallon of berries before leaving the field.

I soon learned, after finding a patch of vines loaded with plump fruit, to fill my bucket quickly and quietly. Only after picking my quota, would I announce the treasure spot to the others,

"Look, here are some big berries."

Such news always brought the other pickers on the run.

Good water flowed from springs at Garretts; one of these supplied our needs for drinking. A private company that furnished water to nearby New Providence, paid a small fee for the water they pulled from a spring at First Hill.

Administration

A Board of Trustees, under the Independent Order of Odd Fellows, Grand Lodge of Tennessee, set the Home's standard. Using his near total power, a superintendent wielded the day to day control. The numbers of paid workers varied from time to time. Besides the superintendent and his wife, the staff included a girls' matron, a kitchen boss, a farm foreman and a band teacher. The boys and girls furnished the farm and household labor, with the old folks often helping with the light work.

Until 1942, when the Home's school, grades 1 through 8, closed, the local Board of Education paid the teachers. After this, we went to public grade school at New Providence. The orphanage did not have a high school — those students attended the public Clarksville High.

Before the start of World War II, many new social laws came on the books. New programs, such as the Social Security System and Aid to Families with Dependent Children, helped reduce the need for the orphanage. These changes trimmed the number of members of the Odd Fellow order. A pickup in business helped this trend. Given the Home's lower census, and the reduced number of new children arriving, the Board of Trustees had few options. They closed the orphanage in 1948, one year after I had finished high school and left. The few children still there either went back to their families or moved to foster homes. The aged people transferred to a nursing home in Nashville.

The Board of Trustees held an auction after it closed the orphanage doors. They sold all the real estate except the graveyard. The record books tell a story. During the 59 years of its existence — some 647 children, aged members and widowed spouses passed through its doors. The Odd Fellows Home had acted as a strong levee holding back the flood waters of pain, hunger and ignorance.

Chapter 3

Chow Time

A blast from the steam whistle at the furnace began the day at six o'clock some thirty minutes after the kitchen girls had started cooking breakfast. A large dinner bell, chiming from its spot near the kitchen door, was audible throughout the farm. It first sounded at 6:30 AM.

Answering the bell's signal, the boys gathered in front of the dining hall. The girls lined up inside the hallway that joined the annex to the main building. Five minutes later a second ring of the bell began breakfast. A line of boys, with the shortest leading, marched military style into the large dining room through the double doors.

We quietly took our places at tables lining the right side of the room. The girls entered through the side door and marched to tables on the opposite side. The tables were large enough to seat ten.

Until everyone reached his or her place we stood behind our chairs in absolute silence. Only then did Mr. Acree issue the next command. He tapped a bell similar to those found on motel counters; this signal meant it was time to say the blessing. From the position behind our chairs, we said grace, using a different blessing for each meal. At breakfast, with heads bowed, we prayed in one voice.

"God is great, God is good and we thank Him for this food, Amen."

We took our seats on the second tap of the bell. A line of girls assigned to do the kitchen work, had been standing at the rear beside a giant six-door refrigerator. They now delivered bowls of hot food to the tables.

The place settings consisted of a fork, knife and spoon plus an aluminum cup, plate and bowl. A dented aluminum pitcher, filled with either milk or molasses according to the day's menu, sat at each end of the table.

Mr. Acree watched our every move and closely supervised the conduct during meals. Every person had to arrive on time. If anyone missed the second dinner bell, he or she could expect a rebuke, or even a more vicious response — something physical. The faces of the boys and girls were somber and low-key while at the table. I loathed these mealtime customs and rules.

If someone spoke too loudly or became rowdy, he or she earned a speedy response from the head table. There, Mr. Acree, along with his wife and two daughters, dined with the band director and matron. If the boss took note of the hubbub, the trouble maker could expect a bit of agony. Mr. Acree might order the young offender to stand at mid-floor, in full view of the entire room. In this way he punished the noisy maker and degraded him before the others.

The table mates often teased the boy, adding to his anguish of standing in the limelight. They tried to shake him from his sober stance. For example, they tried to force him to smile, or even laugh loudly. If the tactic worked, the boy found himself in deeper trouble. When the boss looked somewhere else, we tried to gain the target's attention by making strange faces or giving him the finger of shame. We even pretended to eat the food from his plate.

Although I helped to pester the victim, I knew what it felt like to stand there alone on the hot spot. At those times I hated Mr. Acree's "glare of the limelight" way of causing pain.

The boss rang the bell that ended the meal. Hearing this cue, each person marched out of the dining hall, but first we picked up our dirty dishes and delivered them to a table at the rear.

Working under the charge of the Home's dietitian who also ran the kitchen, the assigned girls bussed the tables, washed the dishes and set the tables for the next meal. They often scrubbed the dining room's wooden floor, and mopped it with pine oil.

The structured routine applied at each meal, but I viewed with pleasure the time we spent dining. In spite of the strict rules, I enjoyed the table chatter with the other boys. I knew that to work with a large number of people required some rules. Still, I hated the part I had to play in Mr. Acree's rigid system of regimentation.

The inequity of mealtime struck me as being most unfair. I often stood behind my chair and brooded about the difference between ours and Mr. Acree's table. The amount, grade and choice of foods "over there" differed from the rations served at our table.

When we ate corn flakes they had bacon, biscuits and gravy. We consumed oatmeal as they satisfied their taste buds with smoked sausage and eggs. We topped our pancakes with white margarine and sorghum molasses, while they dressed theirs with golden butter and honey. We used plates and cups made of aluminum while they dined on china dishes and drank from glass tumblers. This comparison brought feelings of outrage, but this was not my only mealtime problem.

A family could not dine as a unit, because the children sat at tables according to age and gender. The numbers of boys and girls steadily decreased — from about 150 to a dozen, but we still dined according to gender. In the later years, the old folks sat at the head table with the boss. Perhaps a policy that mixed the adults and children at mealtime might have helped both age groups. Mr. Acree's rules didn't allow it.

At times I marched, huffing and puffing, into the dining room just moments before the second bell sounded. Much to my peril, now and then, the bell rang before I was ready to line up. My tardiness caused me to miss supper a few times, but the rule taught me the value of being punctual.

Mr. Acree used the meal period to talk to the group from the head table. He issued special orders to certain people, or maybe he welcomed a boy who had returned for a visit. At times, the boss announced that an important person was to arrive. Forewarned, the pace picked up around the orphanage.

Days before, the work load surged. We swept the sidewalks, mowed the cemetery grounds and cut weeds from the fence rows. We moved the farm tools into the tool shed. Other jobs closer to the living quarters called too: windows needed washing, hallway rugs needed beating, and floors needed scrubbing and mopping. Girls and boys both worked hard at their chores at special times.

When a board member came, all our efforts focused on giving the guest a good impression. A visit by such a person brought more and better food to our tables. We then feasted on more racy items such as smoked ham or sausage, so I didn't mind the extra clean and polish work. A long-winded speech came after the meal, but the better food made a fair enough tradeoff for sitting through the address.

A visit by a lesser person caused no extra work. For example, when a boy returned for a visit our normal daily routine went on.

He dined at the older boys' table, worked in the fields along with the rest of us and engaged in the normal routine. If we baled hay, the visitor did the same. The boss viewed the boy as still living there, but I bestowed an aurora of special status on anyone who had touched the outside world. These visits often felt to me as an older brother had come home.

There were too few of these cases. Our guests seldom stayed for the night, so we gave each one a hearty welcome. Due to the thrill and excitement he brought, we very much enjoyed his company at mealtime. We flocked around the guest and popped the all-important question.

"What's it like out there?"

The tales from the world beyond our front door caught our attention and we listened intently. They filled me with a mixture of hope and anticipation.

We children had little contact with the outside world until our grade school closed, nor did the Home need any scrutiny from without. During those days, neither the State of Tennessee nor the local officials checked on the place. Today, the laws are different. Many states maintain a tight control over their homes for children.

I know of only one case, during my 15-year stay, that an arm of the local government involved itself. Then, it was a matter of health and safety. After the sudden death of a six-year-old girl the safety of our drinking water came into question. The child was not one of us. Her father, a worker at Camp Campbell, had rented and moved the family into the former boys' building.

The tragedy brought people from the health department to check our water. They found that the water was pure, but asked that we install a chlorine system. From a spring at Garretts, we pumped our drinking water through a mile-long, six-inch, cast-iron pipe that leaked often.

A leaky water tank topped a sixty-foot steel tower east of the boys' building. In the winter, when the pressure switch failed to cut off the pump, the wooden tank overflowed, and even longer icicles hung from the structure. Before razing the tower, the Home hired a well digger.

He sank a well near the main building. At three hundred feet he found plenty of water, but it carried a strong order and taste of sulfur. In spite of its bad smell, we received an okay to drink the water.

Each boy and girl received a measure of sulfur from another source every spring. The boss would order the diners at one table to remain seated while the others marched out of the dining hall. We then lined up to receive the spring tonic — a spoon of molasses laced with sulfur. Although we received a yearly dose, I did not know its purpose. I hated it.

Each spring and fall, again without prior notice, we received a dose of Epsom salts. I hated the terrible taste. People those days thought the body needed cleaning out ever so often.

> Each spring and fall, we were given a dose of Epsom salts. I hated the terrible taste.

A dire warning often came with this medicine:

"Don't eat the green apples — let them to hang on the trees until they ripen."

The warning meant nothing to me. If I were the least bit hungry, I ate the green apples direct from the tree. Not once did I suffer the predicted belly cramps. This advice, along with the Epsom salts, came at the mid-day meal instead of at breakfast time.

Our major protein needs came from eggs, pork, cheese, chicken or beef. We produced many of these foods, including the milk served with most meals.

We didn't worry about the lack of pasteurization, even though at times we had a problem with the milk our cows gave. They loved to feed on the bitter weeds and wild onions that grew in the grazing fields each spring. After they ate these plants, the milk's foul odor and bad taste kept us from drinking it. However, the pigs loved it, as did the cat that lived at the barn.

The cat often begged the dairy boys to shoot it a stream of milk directly from the cow's udder. The boys milked the cows twice daily, grossing up to twenty gallons each time, and then hauled the liquid to the dairy room beneath the kitchen.

With the use of a hand-cranked separator, we removed the cream from the whole milk. Most of this cream went for churning butter, but from time to time we used some to make ice cream. At the dining table we drank either buttermilk or skimmed milk. On rare occasions, we converted the skimmed milk into cottage cheese. The hogs drank any surplus or soured milk.

More than any other type of bread, we ate home-baked biscuits, but cornbread ran a close second. I liked both kinds, but the cornbread was more tasty with the addition of cracklings. For Sunday dinner, we often had yeast rolls. Only rarely did we ever see light bread — that is, white bread bought at the store.

Each year we planted and harvested more grain than needed for our consumption. We crushed and fed the surplus wheat, corn and oats to our work animals, including the mules, oxen and horses. The other farm animals, beef and dairy cows, sheep and pigs also ate the grain.

We set aside the wheat and corn for making bread and hauled it six miles to a commercial mill at Ringold, Tennessee. Often using an ox-drawn wagon, we carted the bags of wheat or shelled corn. The miller converted the grain into flour or cornmeal and took his fee from the finished product.

The oxen walked slowly, so a round trip to the mill required an entire day. I enjoyed this journey when the weather was good. That's when we amused ourselves by taking a dip in the mill creek while waiting for our grain.

During one late-fall trip we jumped in for a swim, but the cold water almost ended our fun. The other bigger boys and I swam to the far shore. Meanwhile, Fred jumped in the water wearing his heavy overalls — he had not brought a bathing suit. Fred, the youngest boy in the group, had learned to swim that past summer and tried to keep up.

"Help! Help!"

The tone of his voice told me Fred was in trouble; I looked back. He had reached the deep water at midpoint when he ducked below the surface. He fought his way back to the top as I reached him. I caught the bib of his overalls and he tried to clutch me around neck. While holding him at arm's length, I helped him to the bank. We were lucky that day.

I loved our visits to the mill. That was only one of the means we had to get away from the orphanage for a while, and place didn't matter. We looked forward to every short trip. A ride to the

Clarksville Livestock Market gave another good excuse. Our surplus pigs, beef steers and male calves went to this market, along
with livestock from the other area farms. At times, we rode along
to pick up our supply of staples from the wholesale food dealer.

I was always eager to go. This urge to go somewhere — any-
where — without regard to place reached its peak the year I turned
twelve. The wheat-harvest season was at hand.

I longed to join the thresher crew that stopped at the Home.
Instead of a young boy yearning to join the circus, I saw myself as a
crew member who traveled with the threshing machine. I fanta-
sized; we'd track the harvest season across the country. Starting in
the deep South and moving northward as the fields of grain turned
to amber-gold, we'd end the season in Minnesota. This make-
believe image took me far away from the orphanage and gave me
comfort.

The wheat ripened in mid Summer as the bright green foliage,
dancing in the warm breezes, slowly changed color. The golden
shades told us that it was time to harvest.

Cutting Wheat

We used an antique reaping machine that closely resembled the
original McCormick invention. It contained but few of the features
found in the wheat combines of today. Mules pulled the reaper, but
a few years later our tractor would power it. The machine cut the
wheat, tied it into bundles and dropped them on the ground. Then
the hand labor started.

A line of boys walked behind the machine and picked up the wheat bundles. We stacked a dozen bunches together vertically to make shocks, and then placed two or three bundles across the top to form a roof. The shocked wheat dried several days under the sun.

Shocking Wheat

Although this phase involved some hard work, it opened the prospect for some great fun. We chased wild rabbits, a sport that gave me some of the greatest pleasure of my childhood.

The wheat cutting machine worked from the field's edges toward the center, and the last standing grain. The noise corralled the rabbits inward toward this remaining wheat. The suspense increased with each round. With its cover gone, a rabbit would bolt across the open field toward the fence row. We waited for that moment with searching eyes.

The first boy to sight the fleeing rabbit pointed and yelled at the top of his voice.

"There goes one!"

At this signal, a dozen barefooted boys who had watched from spots scattered around the field, joined in hot pursuit. Back and forth across the field we darted as the wheat stubble scraped against our bare feet.

Someone shouted for our dog to join the chase.

"Go get him, Slum!"

The yell excited our dog, but Slum often couldn't see the target for the stubble. To follow the rabbit she endlessly jumped high into the air, trying to spot it. We zig-zagged across the field in pursuit. Many thrills filled our Summer days, but nothing could equal the sport of running a foot race with a wild rabbit.

The quarry seldom escaped, and this often gave us a chance to eat fried rabbit. The lucky boy who made the catch claimed the choice cut. Of course, he skinned and cleaned the animal before the kitchen girls cooked it.

The wheat threshing machine that moved from farm to farm finally arrived. It would change our routine for the next few days. Pulled behind a smoke-puffing and steam-driven engine, the clumsy giant of a machine slowly rumbled to the wheat field. After picking the exact spot to seat the thresher, we dropped the machine's wheels into holes dug to steady it.

The tractor stood some twenty feet away and sent power to the threshing machine through a flat drive belt. From the loaded wagons, pulled out of the fields by oxen and mules, we fed the dried bundles of wheat into the hopper. This part of the harvest was hot, dirty, and at times proved to be dangerous.

One day, as I hoisted the bundles of wheat onto a wagon, a brownish colored snake slithered down my pitchfork handle. For an instant the copperhead and I glared at each other, eye to eye. I quickly gave both the pitchfork and wheat to the culprit. Snakes, as did the wild rabbits, often found shelter inside the shocks of drying wheat. Although the snake frightened me, we soon killed the reptile.

The machine belched the stalks of wheat and chaff through a long metal pipe onto a straw stack, meanwhile, the kernels dropped into a burlap bag. Filling and tying off these bags of wheat kept one boy busy. One day as we threshed wheat the large straw stack caught fire. The blaze gave off a torrid heat and spread rapidly through the bone-dry straw. The machine's crew quickly hooked up the tractor and pulled the big thresher to safety without injury.

Except for this one fiery case, we baled the straw and used it throughout the year to line the animal stalls. Each spring, we removed the manure from the barn and scattered it on the fields. This made a good fertilizer for the crops.

Besides the grain, we grew many good things to eat. The cook, dietitian and kitchen boss, Miss Noah Anderson, saw to the content of our diet. She based most meals on the home-grown fruits or vegetables on hand, or perhaps a butchered animal. If we had just killed hogs, for example, she might build the meal around pork backbone and sauerkraut. The diet changed with the seasons.

The home-grown items I liked best, often eating them in the field, were turnips, carrots and Irish potatoes. We dined on many other items from our summer garden, including peas, okra and squash. Other treats such as beans, turnip greens and sweet potatoes graced out dining table. We raised chickens, using them for both frying and for their eggs. The turkeys we had raised often wound up on our holiday table.

Just before the first frost of the Fall, we picked the green tomatoes still on the vines, wrapped them in brown paper and stored them in the cool basement. They often lasted for six weeks, or until Thanksgiving Day.

We seldom dined on produce that was out of season those days. Few cargo-cooled trucks supplied the local markets with fruits and produce grown in warmer climates. We either consumed the items fresh from the garden or preserved the over-supply for later use when we could not use them at harvest time.

Other than the cultivated items, we picked large amounts of wild blackberries and made jam or jelly. We canned the home grown vegetables and fruits using both gallon and half-gallon glass jars. On one occasion we put up nine bushels of peaches. Such canning allowed us to enjoy the seasonal items throughout the year.

Certain days brought a variety of special foods. The Fourth of July was one of those days. On that occasion we barbecued a hog, a small steer, and sometimes a goat or sheep. After preparing a pit near the baseball diamond, we started the cooking around midday on July 3. A rack made by stretching fence wire across iron pipes, held the meat above a pit of hot embers. A bonfire of hickory wood furnished the coals for the pit.

We transferred these live coals to the pit throughout the day, evening and night, making sure not to build up too much heat under the meat. Well-cooked barbecued called for a low heat. The boy in charge of the task turned the meat repeatedly, and each time, painted it with a sauce made of ground hot peppers, vinegar and salt. As a youngster I always enjoyed this scene, and often stood nearby until deep into the night of July third.

By midday of the Fourth, the meat was ready for the picnic. The spicy sauce made the barbecue hot, but that did not stop us from eating our fill of the tasty and tender morsels. The gala involved a feast served from a long makeshift table, followed by a baseball game.

In late Summer, at this site near the ball diamond, we pressed juice from sugar cane and turned it into molasses. As with the barbecue, the superintendent assigned a senior boy as "straw boss." His job was to see that the project went well.

When we made molasses it required teamwork, as several jobs had to go on at the same time. It started by our stripping the leaves from the cane as it stood in the field, cutting the stalks and hauling them to the press. Three boys fed stock into the mill, kept the mule moving and hauled away the crushed stalks. One boy poured the raw juice into the cooker pan, while another chopped the wood and maintained a roaring fire under it. The senior boy, and others charged with the actual cooking, ended the process at just the right time. That's when they scooped the tasty molasses into shiny new one gallon cans.

Although the job called for hard work, I loved the aroma of molasses as it cooked. First, the sugar cane passed through the iron rollers of a press machine that reminded me of a giant laundry wringer turned on its side. A mule, hitched to the end of a long pole, powered the rig by plodding in an endless circle path.

The cane stalks entered the machine round and came out flat, and the juice dropped into a five-gallon bucket. We poured the buckets of sweet, but cloudy, green liquid into the hottest end of the galvanized cooker pan. A blazing fire brought the juice to a frothy boil and drove clouds of sweet-smelling, white steam into the air. The pan measured five feet wide, twelve feet long and nine inches deep. It had partitions spaced at eight-inch gaps in a criss-cross pattern that directed the path of the juice as it cooked.

The boys slowly worked the cooking juice from side to side and pushed it toward the end of the pan. They used metal scoops mounted to the ends of long wooden handles to skim off the frothy scum. The juice gradually lost its initial color and turned to a translucent brown as it approached the finish.

I liked to make molasses although it was hard work. The payback would come later. Sinking one's teeth into a hot, buttered biscuit smothered in molasses, made it all seem worthwhile. Molasses was only one of the many tasty foods I enjoyed.

Our most hardy meal came at noon between the morning and afternoon rounds in the fields. We called this dinner. Our work schedule called for much energy, so we needed all the help we could get to make it through the day. At eleven-thirty the dinner bell summoned us from the fields and the steam whistle sounded promptly at noon. This gave us thirty minutes to walk from the fields and wash up before entering the dining room. We generally were back at work again by one o'clock.

I was never truly hungry, for the Home's food was adequate. A growing boy, however, often thinks he needs food between meals. If I felt the least bit hungry, I looked for something to eat. Fruit from the orchard trees, raw vegetables from the garden or fresh milk from the cows often filled my supposed needs. I especially liked dry cereal topped with strawberries, sweetened and bathed in whole milk. Due to my almost constant eating, I gained a 20 pound surplus and kept it on between the age of nine and fourteen.

One day, my brother Fred said,

"I'm starved Buddy. Let's see if we can find something to eat."

The pantry, located off the kitchen, held the often-used supplies such as flour and lard. The cook stored the other bulky food stocks in a basement room behind a padlocked door. This was no match for the hunger pangs of two growing boys. Fred and I resolved to explore the food items preserved in glass jars or metal cans that lined the shelves of this storage room.

We wanted a taste of the honey stashed in the pantry, so we looked for a way to gain access. I checked the room's back door with a flashlight, and then whispered,

"Look at this Fred; someone has had this panel out. No one will ever know we came in this way after we put it back in place."

The panel popped out easily.

"Here — hold the light while I go in."

The opening was too small for me to pass through.

Fred offered.

"You're too big to get through there. Let me try it,"

He easily slid through the opening as I waited outside. Beaming the light around the room, he spotting several large cans on the wooden shelves.

"Here's some honey," Fred said as he passed a gallon tin through the opening. He snaked himself out of the dark room, and I replaced the door panel to cover our tracks. We retreated to a safe piece in the basement to enjoy the spoils of our raid. I pried the lid off the can.

"Look what's in this can — it's nothing but gooey stuff."

The contents, had started as sorghum molasses, but had turned into a gritty sugary-like substance.

"We can't eat that stuff. It must have sat on the shelf for over two years, but what are we going to do with it?" Fred asked.

"Let's put it back and try to find something that we can eat."

Fred passed through the opening a second time. He replaced the gallon can of bad molasses and whispered to me,

"How about some tomato juice?"

I took the gallon jar of home-canned juice. The red solids had settled at the bottom, leaving a clear liquid at the top. I shook the jar vigorously, opened it and took a sip. We drank our fill of tomato juice.

My assignment made food finding easy — I worked as the kitchen boy between the ages of 9 and 13. My hunger pangs seldom lasted until the next meal; I ate too well.

The same system of signal bells that rang for breakfast and dinner also began the march into the dining room for the evening meal. We called this meal supper.

Our Sunday evening meal differed both in content and style from the other days. It consisted of two sandwiches — peanut butter and soda crackers — plus a piece of fruit. At times, cheese replaced the peanut butter and a cookie or a piece of gingerbread replaced the fruit.

On Saturday afternoons, the girls would wrap the meal in wax paper and pack it in a brown paper bag. Since this took place more than 24 hours before supper time on Sunday, it's little wonder that the crackers had become soggy and limp.

This meal taught me to hate peanut butter. Too often, as I tried to eat it, the moist crackers and gooey mess would cling to the roof of my mouth. I did, however, enjoy one thing about the Sunday supper. It was the only meal without our having to go through the formal routine of marching into dining room.

We received the brown bag at the midday meal, but we could eat it when and where we pleased. The other boys and I often made good use of this privilege; we took our paper-bag suppers to Garretts. For me, hiking in the woods or along the brook without supervision was the closest thing to freedom.

Besides this good effect, the Sunday supper gave me some problems. One had to do with my early years at the orphanage and my daily chore. Starting at age six, I was charged with keeping the front lawn free of debris. Those brown paper bags and waxed paper wrappers had a knack for showing up on my lawn on Monday mornings. If I missed one piece of trash, the boss called on me to explain why I'd fallen down on my job.

The students took their lunch to high school. Like the Sunday supper, it was peanut-butter and crackers in a paper bag. Its contents embarrassed me, a sensitive teenager. Instead of eating the meal with classmates, I looked for an out-of-sight, private place. I often ate lunch in the boys' room.

With fewer and fewer people living at the Home, the strict order at meal time began to relax. After Mr. Acree left, the practice of bell ringing ended — much to my delight. The young and old, and male and female, dined at two tables without hassle. The only routine to survive the change was the custom of saying grace at each meal. During my last years, our chow time moved to the kitchen.

Mr. Acree's leaving and the new bosses' reforms had put me at ease. Mr. A. S. Byrom, our last superintendent, made the most positive steps. Through his leadership, and with help from the Tennessee Odd Fellow Grand Lodge, our fortunes changed. Each high-school-aged boy and girl received a small weekly allowance. We could now go to the cafeteria, buy lunch and join our classmates without the stigma of the brown paper bag.

Chapter 4

Work Detail

Saturday morning, Mr. Acree stood on the porch of the boys' building and blew "assembly." Every boy in the work force knew that this blast from the army bugle meant a call to action — it ordered us to the office at once. The boss was ready to hand out job assignments. To ignore this summons, coming soon after breakfast, was the same as asking for trouble.

I moved to the small boys' dorm and joined the work force in 1934, the year I reached my sixth birthday. This meant that I worked alongside the other boys. When the bugle called, I headed straight for Mr. Acree's office on the first floor.

One entered the front door into a large hallway. Two doors on the right opened to the school's classrooms. To the left, beyond a large entrance to the auditorium, a stairway led to the second-floor dorms. The office was at the rear of the hall. Near the office door, beneath the staircase, a door opened to the basement below. The hall's wooden floors glistened and smelled of the pine oil used when mopping.

Four windows, reaching nearly to the ceiling, covered most of the office's rear wall. From this vantage point, the boss had a grand view of the rear grounds. He could see the garage, baseball field and dairy barn. A large, roll-top desk sat at the far right corner. It had dozen pigeonholes that held folded letters. The boss sat at the desk in a wooden chair that squeaked when it swiveled.

A picture of George Washington hung on the wall above the desk. The founding father wore a vague look on his face that resembled a male Mona Lisa. Mr. Acree often wore that stony face when he handed out the work assignments. All business, he seldom smiled and quickly changed his expression if he became angry. His mood always showed in his face, and he never tried to conceal his rage.

One Saturday morning soon after I entered the work force, I joined some 25 other boys making their way toward the office. An electric tension filled the air. Three teenage boys worried that a problem with the boss would rupture and cause them to suffer. They huddled in the hallway before going in the office. Speaking in a hushed voice, one of the three said,

"He knows, I saw her father leave the office last night."

It seems that a neighbor girl had made some false charges against the boys. She had told her father that they cursed and made unkind remarks about her as she walked home from school. He had brought the matter to Mr. Acree. Since the boys were not guilty, they had decided between themselves that if the boss so much as laid a hand on one of them, they would defend each other.

I walked into the office and looked for a place to sit. There were too few chairs to seat everyone, so I sat with several other boys on the steps leading to a narrow mezzanine. A wooden guardrail extended up along the steps. Shelves filled with books lined the balcony that jutted out from the room's upper left and front walls. Bookcases with glass front panels also covered an area below the steps and around much of the office lower wall space.

Several boys sat in folding chairs, and six others sat in cane-bottom chairs around a center table. The only light was a single light bulb, supported by a green twisted cord, hanging in the center of the room. Mr. Acree's face blazed with anger, and everyone expected some sort of action. Rising from his swivel chair, he stood before the oldest of the three boys,

"You know better than to curse, especially when girls are around. The neighbor was here and told me that you three boys shouted foul words at his daughter yesterday."

"But we —"

"I don't want to hear it," shouted Mr. Acree as he stepped toward the nearest boy.

Before the boy was able to deny the accusation the boss grabbed him by the bib of his overalls, pulled him to his feet and raised an open hand to strike him.

The boy pushed Mr. Acree backward and blurted,

"You're done hitting me!"

The two other teenagers jumped to their feet and joined the first as the boss tried to regain his footing. A chair used by one boy at the table overturned and shattered the glass front of a bookcase.

We gasped at the act of defiance. The three continued to push the boss in the direction of the stairs where we sat. We jumped out of the way as they came nearer.

Crack!

A loud report came as the boss fell against the handrail and to the floor. The boys came forward as if to continue when he stood up. Realizing that he was losing control, the boss yelled,

"That's enough of this."

Obviously caught off guard by the clash, Mr. Acree picked himself up, returned to his desk and dropped into the squeaky swivel chair. The noise of the pushing match lapsed into dead silence. No one spoke a word, but the tension remained. With glaring eyes, Mr. Acree searched the room. He fixed a stare on each boy as if to find the extent of our involvement. Time slowed — stood still. The tension seemed to hang for hours, although the angry stares lasted no more than a few moments.

The tension slowly abated. Finally, the boss rose from his seat to inspect the wreckage. Except for the broken glass and ruined banister, the brawl had caused little other damage. To the pleasure of every boy present, the incident seemed to have shattered Mr. Acree's pride and prestige. Untouched by the physical outbreak, I silently cheered when it looked as if the boys had won the conflict. At least, Mr. Acree whipped no one that morning.

The feeling of triumph didn't last long. Before noon, two squad cars stopped in front of the building and sheriff's deputies got out. They took the three boys to the county jail and kept them there overnight.

For the next several days thereafter, we younger boys enjoyed some fun at the expense of the three:

"Hello jail bird," I said to one of them. This was the first time I used the term in his presence.

He looked me in the eye and said,

"Look Buddy, I can't make you shut up, but I sure can make you wish you had." I grasped his meaning — my fun-poking ended at once.

In spite of this revolt, the boys who grew up at the orphanage took their place in the world as lawful people. Mr. Acree had good reason to create fear in the minds of the boys. It served his purpose by allowing him to retain control. This kept us on the right course — I know of only one case in which a boy turned out wrong.

This fellow had left the orphanage soon after we arrived. He stole some items from a store that his family owned and landed in jail. Mr. Acree intervened, gained the boy's parole and brought him back to the Home. A few months later the boy ran away from the orphanage and traveled North. Some two years later, he stole a car. One evening under the cover of darkness, he arrived and asked the dairy boys to help him stay out of sight for a few days. The police were on his trail. Soon every boy knew of the clandestine guest in the barn's hayloft; some brought him food. He rested in the safe haven for only a couple of days.

The local sheriff suspected that he might visit us, so the deputies showed up and searched the entire area. Too late, our secret boarder had left the night before. We neither saw nor heard from the former resident again.

I left had the nursery to join the older boys at work in the fields only a few weeks before the office conflict. Mr. Acree matched the demands of a particular job with the boy who had the needed skill and strength. He gave me the first job of work in the fields. I was to act as the water boy.

That first day we walked to a spot on the Red River, a half-mile up stream from the Cumberland River. This was near the place that highway 41W crossed the Red River. The orphanage did not own this bottom land. We worked it as sharecroppers.

A dozen boys with hoes, spread out in a line across the field, slowly worked their way along the long rows of corn. Every now and then a worker stooped over to pull by hand the weeds that grew too close to the corn. Plowing offered help little against the unwanted Johnson grass that grew next to the corn stalks. The young corn and grass looked so much alike that I wondered how the boys knew which to chop. The grass, growing much faster than the corn, offered some tough competition to the boys and their hoes.

A hot sun beamed down on the line of workers as they inched their way along the rows. Their shirts were wet with sweat by mid morning. My job began, but I needed both hands to lug the galvanized bucket of drinking water. As I approached each boy, he stopped hoeing, took the dipper made from a gourd and scooped a drink of water from my bucket. I made many trips across the corn field throughout the day.

During my second day on the job, a teenager with sweat dripping from his brow, took the gourd and flashed me a smile. He said,

"Thanks, Buddy. Since I don't know your name, I'll just call you Buddy."

Hoeing Corn

The tag stuck. Soon all at the orphanage, except Miss Frances the teacher, called me Buddy. Years later, as I prepared to leave, I linked the nickname with the place and wanted to forget that label completely. I asked a special favor of my brother and sisters. I told Fred, Barbara and June that I wished to leave "Buddy" behind in Clarksville with all those bad memories. Thankfully, they honored the request.

Through the years, the boss assigned me to do many types of work. Some were fun; one of these jobs came each Summer when we filled the silo. We harvested the stalks of sugar cane and corn and fed them into a tractor-powered hammer mill. This machine chopped the stems and leaves into bits and blew them through a large metal tube over the top and down into the silo. I liked the inside work, aiming the flexible blow pipe to layer the material.

The silage gave off a pleasant aroma in the summer when freshly chopped. By the winter, when we fed the cows, it reeked of a sharp pungent, or fermented, odor. The cows seemed to love this tartness caused by the curing process. They begged for it and rushed to eat the stuff when we fed them.

Other jobs weren't as much fun. During the cleaning rituals of each spring and fall, Mr. Acree assigned us beat the rugs. Having no vacuum sweeper in those days, we rolled up the carpets, carried them outside and draped them over a clothesline. Using three-foot-long heavy wire beaters, we pounded until the cloud of dust stopped flying. Only then, did we return the rugs to the halls and rooms in the main building.

This job represented only a small part of the cleaning routine. Each spring, the girls thoroughly cleaned every inch of space inside the kitchen and dining room. The boys washed the windows and hung the screens that we had taken down for the winter. We cleaned out the animal stalls at the dairy and horse barns. Spring and summer were our busy seasons.

These side jobs represented only a small part of the total work. Most of our manual labor had to do with the farm. Endless boy-hours of effort gave us a near self-sufficiency in food production.

The boys, ranging from 6 to 18 years old, furnished the required muscle power of the farm. Much of this effort flowed through the handle of a hoe, pitchfork or weed cutter. We used these tools without the blister protection of gloves. At the beginning of each season our hands soon toughened, but not before painful blisters had formed and burst.

Many of these jobs required a high level of labor due to the ancient farming methods we used. For example, a mule-drawn mower cut the clover or alfalfa hay. After the crop had dried in the sun, a mule-pulled rake rolled the hay into parallel rows. The rake then straddled the row. The driver kicked the control lever from time to time to lift the giant circle tongs that formed piles of hay. We hand loaded the loose hay on to wagons. The oxen, mules or horses pulled the loads to the barn. Using the pitchforks again, we hoisted the hay to the storage place in the loft.

In early summer the mules pulled plows along rows of tender corn; this added dirt to the roots and killed the rival weeds. The two-legged animals, dressed in bib overalls, worked almost as hard as the four-legged beasts. The boys guided the plows, hoed the weeds and harvested the corn by hand.

We used some machinery on the farm, but our wheat reaper needed much hand labor to help harvest the crop. Boys, walking behind the machine, picked up the bundles of wheat and placed them into stacks for drying.

Although later on a tractor powered our hay bailer, we had to bring the hay or straw to the machine. We set the length of the bale by putting a wooden divider between each unit. As the machine compacted the hay, a boy slid the bailing wire through the wooden block's grooves and hand-tied the wire. The bailer's springs fixed the bale's weight. We loaded the heavy bales of hay on the wagon and stacked them in the barn's loft by hand.

The steel spikes mounted on the early model tractor gave it better traction. The Farmall tractor pulled several types of farm implements used for tilling the soil. They included a plow for turning the sod, compactor for breaking the clods of dirt and scratch harrow for smoothing the land. Even when we used these machines, much of our farm work depended on our hand labor.

Much of the work took place in the hot sun, but the nature and extent of the jobs changed with the season. We put out a garden in the spring, and made hay during the summer. In the fall we dug sweet potatoes and in the winter killed hogs. We made watermelon rind preserves, picked and canned tomatoes or gathered and shelled corn. We always had plenty of work, and the farm called for many types of jobs.

Mr. Acree assigned the boys to clean the chicken house, cut tall saplings for making bean poles or whitewash the front lawn trees. We picked up rocks from the fields and placed them in gullies to prevent soil erosion. By cleaning out the barn stables and spreading the manure on the fields, we fertilized the crops and improved the land.

The growing of crops took most of our efforts. The wheat, corn and hay crops gave some added income when a good season helped to bring yields beyond our own needs. We sheared sheep and sold the wool, but tobacco brought in more cash.

All kinds of farm plants need attention, but tobacco calls for more than the others. Each year's crop requires thirteen months of effort. Our work began in December when we prepared a plant bed. It ended over a year later when we hauled the crop to the a uction warehouse at Clarksville. The orphanage was in an area of good tobacco farmland, and we raised two kinds of the plant.

Burley tobacco leaves turn from green to a light tan, or dull yellow, as they air-dry. One use of the this type is to make cigar wrappers. The second type, or dark-fired tobacco, has a heavy leaf that requires heat in its curing process. This plant dries to a darker brown color and is more likely to end up as cigarettes. We dried our crop by hanging it in the barn and burning wood for heat.

To start the tobacco each year, we picked a fertile site for a seed bed at Garretts. After clearing the trees and brush from a fresh spot, we raked the combustible debris on the bed and lit a bonfire. The heat killed any weed seeds and disinfected the soil.

We tilled the burned area, sowed it with the tiny tobacco seeds and stretched a cheesecloth over the logs that lined the edge. This shielded the tender sprouts from damage by a late cold snap. Within a few days, the bright green plants shot up from the black soil. Each tender seedling vied for its share of nutrient, moisture and sunlight.

In early summer, when they had reached a height of six to eight inches, we pulled the shoots from the bed. They were ready for setting out in the tobacco patch. Meanwhile we broke the ground, smoothed the field with a disk harrow and used a plow and a mule to lay out parallel rows. We made a hole for each plant, poured in a pint of water and set each one by hand.

The tobacco began to grow, and so did the weeds. We hoed the weeds and cultivated the crop walking along the rows behind a mule and plow. When the plants had grown to about a foot tall, suckers popped out on the stalk above each leaf. These we removed by hand. Near the end of the growing season the tobacco flowered; we then snapped the top off each plant.

More than any other job in growing the crop, the one I hated most had to do with the control of tobacco worms. These three-inch long, fat and juicy, culprits assumed the exact color of the plant on which they fed. The camouflage green made our work difficult. We had to search for the worms, hand-pick them from the leaves and mash off their heads.

The thought of those worms crawling on the leaves turned my stomach and made me resolve never to smoke cigarettes. The aftermath of my first and only try at smoking helped me keep my resolution. I was twelve that fall day when a friend dared me to smoke a homemade cigar. I took the dare. I would smoke not one, but two. He plucked the tan leaves from the bottom of a burley plant standing in the field, crushed them and rolled the tobacco in brown paper. Acting like a seasoned smoker, I lit the first fat stogie and drew the smoke into my lungs.

My first reaction was to cough, cough, and cough. Should I quit? Of course not, a dare is a dare. Once under way, I continued to smoke even though my head began to spin. I stubbornly finished both of the hand-rolled cigars. My body, unaccustomed to the tar and nicotine, reacted badly to the assault. They said I turned a light shade of green, and I was sick for the next several days. No more smokes for me, thank you.

A few weeks after the incident, I had a talk in the dorm with Quentin Perry. He was my junior by one year. Pulling a clump of tobacco from his pocket, Quentin broke off a piece and popped it into his mouth. When I saw this, I told him how tobacco sickness had tortured me.

He said with a chuckle,

"You just can't take it, that's why you got sick. Tobacco don't bother me one bit."

"I bet you can't take it either, let's just see," I replied. I cupped my hand over his mouth.

Being the larger, I was able to keep him from spitting out the tobacco juice. The scuffle brought us both on the floor. He finally swallowed some of the tobacco juice and I let him up. Quentin turned green too. Afterward as we worked the crop, he could have chewed tobacco on many occasions, but he had lost the desire.

Burley tobacco ripens slowly from the bottom of the plant up as it changes to a light shade of yellow brown. At harvest time, using a curve-blade knife, we split the plant's stem from the top down to within eight inches of the bottom before cutting it just above the ground. We hung six plants on six-foot long tobacco sticks. To prevent leaf damage, we allowed the crop to wilt in the sun for two hours before hauling and hanging it the barn.

Each of the two tobacco types, dark-fired and burley, required its own curing process. We dried the harvested dark-fired, or flue-cured, variety with a fire burning on the barn's dirt floor. As the heat increased the fat green worms that escaped being picked in the field began to drop. They struck the barn's dirt floor with a plop — plop, slowly at first. Then the tempo quickened to sound like giant raindrops pounding the earth at the start of a summer shower.

The plants hung in the barn through November. Once cured, during a day of high humidity, we stripped the leaves from the stalks and sorted them into piles of light, medium, or dark shades. The leaves, when graded according to color, brought a higher price at the warehouse. The auctioneers strolled along rows of flat baskets filled with bright leaves and yelled their mumble jumble. The buyers understood the jargon, but I didn't.

Our work had not ended, even after we had delivered the tobacco to market. The stalks still contained useful nutrients, so we spread them on the lawn's weakest spots or on the barren red clay zones of the fields. The winter rains leached the fertile tidbits from the stems into the soil and promoted growth of the grass or plants.

Finally, we removed the stalks from the lawn or field and hauled them to a nearby washed-out gully. This helped to prevent soil erosion that came with the spring rains. As with each crop, more than 12 months had passed since we burned the plant bed at Garretts.

Meanwhile, there was plenty of other work. Mr. Acree stayed abreast of the farm concerns that most needed attention and assigned the must-do tasks. In a few cases, he could find no pressing farm job, but as any farmer knows, this seldom happens. During these times the boss thought up other ways to keep us busy.

One day, for example, he said, "I want you boys to hitch the oxen to the wagon, go to the field beyond the chicken house and pick up rocks. We need to do something about that gully in the next field."

The white rocks near the hilltop stood out against a background of red clay dirt. Although we regularly picked up the exposed stones, more showed up each time we cultivated the field.

Easy to spot, they ranged from football sized downward. One day we filled a wagon with rocks and hauled them some two hundred yards to the next field. We planned to unload them at the spot where we had thrown tree limbs and other trash to control erosion.

Arriving at the gully before the others, I heard a rustle in the limbs of a discarded Christmas tree. I called for the other boys to help me check to see if we had cornered a rabbit. Our dog, Slum, joined the search as we charged down into the ravine from both sides.

A small animal stirred, but it was no rabbit. With a well-aimed blast, a skunk defended itself against three boys and a dog. Since Slum had arrived first, the dog received the strongest blast. We all reeked with the sharp smelling, foul odor.

We ran home, took off our clothes and showered repeatedly, but the odor lingered even after all the scrubbing. Since we still reeked with the obnoxious smell that evening, everyone avoided us. We ate supper outside on the kitchen porch steps. Our clothes passed through several washing cycles before we were able to wear them; and no one allowed Slum near him for days.

Picking and hauling away the rocks helped to cure the land, but there was another way to improve the bad spots. This we did by spreading many loads of manure. This material came from cleaning out the horse stables and dairy-cow stalls. The effort built up the poor soil, but the pungent odors abused one's sense of smell.

One work detail, however, helped to balance these bad aromas. This job involved our cleaning the sweet smelling honeysuckle vines and other growth from the fence rows. It required the use of axes, grub hoes and cutting blades, or 'Lively Lads,' our name for the tool used to cut tall weeds. The saplings, hollyhocks and morning glories also clogged the fence rows. Farming involved many kinds of labor.

We learned to farm by watching the older boys and the straw boss. Years before our family arrived, Mr. York, a superintendent during the 1920's, started the chain of schooling. Then, the farm-land was less than standard and required much improvement. He asked the Home's board to hire an agricultural mentor. Working for only two years, the expert taught the boys and superintendent how to use the best farming methods. They, in turn, passed this skill down to the later residents.

Although Mr. Acree knew how to farm, he often gave out jobs just to keep us busy. One day he said,

"Joe, you and Buddy hitch the mules to double shovels and plow the cornfield down by the lower orchard."

The time had long passed when such cultivation would add value to the corn crop. The ears had matured enough to eat as corn-on-the-cob. Without questioning the boss's order, we plowed the corn. We not only drove the animals and guided the plows, but also dodged the big ears of corn passing our heads.

Besides the normal farm work, the boss assigned every boy over the age of six a special task. These fixed chores called for our full attention; they played an important role in our lives. Mr. Acree checked each person's task throughout the day, making sure that we did the chore on time.

Not even the slightest detail about the special chore failed to escape his sharp eyes. Our duties, at which we worked both before and after school, ranked above all other things. My first job was to keep a portion of the lawn clean. Mr. Acree could easily observe my work, as my section was directly in front of the main building. He checked my labor, or lack of it, several times daily. I soon learned the value of obeying orders and doing my job.

The boss assigned my brother Fred to the dairy, where each morning and evening he helped milk the cows. With practice he became highly skilled at the job. After a short time on the job, he could quickly fill his milk bucket and keep up with the bigger boys.

Each girl also worked at a specific job. It might involve tending the flowers, working in the kitchen or cleaning a given section of a hallway, dorm or dining room. Twice weekly, they fired up the laundry facility. Besides these assigned jobs, they canned fruits and garden products in season. Mrs. Acree, with the help of a hired matron, saw that the girls did their part. A dietitian oversaw those assigned to do the kitchen work and dining room chores.

Mr. Acree often assigned an older boy to act as the boss in his absence. This person, known as the straw boss, took charge and saw to it that the others performed the day's assigned work. For example, one senior boy held the job of caring for the dairy. Mr.

Widgery, who took over from Mr. Acree, hired a farm supervisor to work full time. Mr. Williamson was the farm boss for about a year.

When Mr. Williamson left, Dewey James, himself brought up at the Home, hired on as our farm boss. Dewey, who had just returned from a wartime tour in the U. S. Army, worked hard and was a tough task master.

A matter arose to become a threat to his life before the new straw boss had been on the job very long. One day we had cut hay and left it in the sun to dry until the next day. Only Dewey, Fred and I worked with the hay. After raking it into piles, we hauled the loose hay from the field and loaded it into the barn loft from the wagon.

Fred heaved the hay into the loft. Like a bucket brigade moving hay instead of water, I tossed each batch on to Dewey. He then moved the hay in its final storage spot. From time to time, the three of us changed position. The problem began as we worked on the second load.

We used the pitch forks without gloves, but our hands had not yet callused. This was the first time we had used pitchforks that season. Without protection, the blisters had popped up where our tender hands rubbed the pitchfork handles.

A large water bubble on Fred's palm had ruptured, and the sweat had made the problem worse. He stopped for a moment to nurse a sore hand, and said

"My blisters hurt."

Dewey, seeing that Fred had stopped work, shouted a military-toned order,

"Don't slow down now. Let's get this wagon unloaded."

"But my hand hurts."

"We don't have time for you to gold-brick," Dewey snapped.

Without another word, Fred hoisted the next load of hay to my feet. This time, however, he allowed the pitchfork to sail up with the hay. He jumped from the wagon to the wall-mounted ladder and climbed to the loft.

I thought he wanted to change jobs with me, but Fred said nothing. He stepped from the ladder, grabbed his pitchfork and headed straight for Dewey. His stern look confirmed his intent as he drew back into a threatening pose.

Dewey's eyes lit up when he saw that Fred aimed to do him harm. I rushed toward Fred, arriving just in time. Before he made the jab, I grabbed the rear end of the drawn-back pitchfork and held the handle with all my strength. Fred wheeled around and flashed a look of surprise.

I had never seen any one so driven. Twelve years old at the time, Fred soon cooled down.

Fortunately, he failed to complete the thrust. A shaken Dewey, sensing that the danger had passed, allowed a respite for Fred to attend the blisters that gloves could have prevented.

We wore bib overalls and a blue cotton shirt when doing this type of farm work. During the hot months we wore no shoes, but preferred to go barefoot. The girls wore straight, sleeveless cotton dresses that extended well below the knee.

During my early days at the orphanage, all clothes were common property. The garments issued to the children on Saturday afternoons were theirs for a week's use. In later years, with fewer boys and girls, this policy changed.

My spirits soared when I first wore garments that belonged only to me. Later, by the time I started high school, June and Barbara looked after our clothes. June ironed Fred's shirts and Barbara ironed mine. From time to time they rotated.

Every boy and girl, whether in the laundry or on the farm, worked hard. This labor sparked a state of mind that became a major milestone in my life. I was thirteen. We were cutting and shocking corn on a sultry day in August day.

When dry, the edges of the corn leaves are sharp as a razor. This can inflict an injury like that from the sharp edge of paper. Rivulets of sweat poured from my brow, and the salt stung my arms and hands where the leaves had ripped the skin. I reviewed my life. My thoughts went back across the nine years I'd lived at the orphanage.

Mentally, I suffered anew through the work and the pain it caused over the years. I thought, "Is this what I can expect from a life outside the orphanage?" There must be a better way to make a living than by doing this hard farm work.

Would my fate include nothing more than manual labor? Yes, unless I did something to change the path I traveled. I saw myself drifting in the wrong direction. Perhaps I should aim for a brighter future, one without the hard labor. As I thought about the contrasting futures, a new idea appeared. The tomorrow that I would face depended on what I had done, or had not done. With that thought in mind, the choice between the two courses grew easier.

In the midst of the heat, sweat and misery, I resolved never to become a farmer. I loathed cutting and shocking corn; I hated farm work. During my short life, I had already seen more than enough of this manual labor. "Once I begin to make my own way, things will be different. I'll earn a living with brain power instead of brawn power."

> Overcome by the heat, sweat and misery, I resolved never to become a farmer.

When this new insight came to me, the country had begun a troop buildup. Several boys from the orphanage had answered the draft call. A tune about the new soldiers popped into my head. It boomed over the radio daily:

"You're in the Army now,
You're not behind a plow.
You can't get rich
By digging a ditch,
You're in the Army now."

The melody burned an image into my psyche, but I had no thoughts of joining the Army. The lyrics spoke to me about my life at the orphanage. The phrases, "Behind a plow and digging a ditch," were the focal points of my juvenile mind. I longed for a better life in the future — one without the hard work.

To avoid such a life, or that of a farmer, I'd needed to set myself some goals. I must learn to use my brain to escape a life driven by brawn power. These musings prompted the daydreams that helped me to come up with a set of some long-term goals. With the help of many people, and the passage of time, the details began to jell. I must learn a trade or profession after leaving the orphanage. To make all this come true, I needed to draw up some plans.

The painful sweat on that hot summer day in the corn field had given me a purpose. The thought of a future filled with labor gave me the needed thrust. I would go to college. With the help of Superintendent Byrom and a few high school teachers, I set my sights on gaining an education.

Chapter 5

Superintendents

Mr. Grey Acree

"This should keep you boys at home," said Mr. Acree as he shoved my brother Fred and me in the broom closet and bolted the door behind us. Two types of darkness enveloped me; one was the black reality of the room and the other my mental state. My eyes soon adjusted to the tiny sliver of light that sneaked under the door, but my bad feeling remained.

More than three hours passed before the sounds of stomping feet drifted into our dark jail. The noise from overhead and outside the door ended a lengthy silence during which neither Fred nor I had spoken. The area soon buzzed with the clamor of giggling girls. They had assembled in the hall between the main building and the dining facility. At any moment, the bell would ring and start the girls marching to the supper table.

Our makeshift jail beneath the stairs served as a storage room for mops, brooms and cleaning supplies. The steps above us led to the girls' dorm. They formed a low ceiling at the back of the closet. The nearest thing to a seat in the cramped space was a mop bucket, but a foot wringer made its use as a seat almost hopeless.

Fred was seven years old at the time and I was ten. Mr. Acree had bolted Fred in this room on prior occasions, but this was my first lockup. After we spent most of the afternoon in the dark, the telltale noise told us supper time was at hand.

I wondered — would Mr. Acree soon release us? Although hunger pangs gnawed at my stomach, my main thought was my imprisonment. I desperately wanted out of the room. Throughout the long afternoon I had hidden my fear from Fred. An inner voice calmed me with, "Don't let the dark scare you." While trying not to worry my little brother, I recalled the events that led to our detention.

Fred and I, soon after the mid-day meal, had seen some new kids in the area. Since Mr. Acree had driven away in the pickup truck, we felt free to walk over and talk with these youngsters. We crossed our turnip field, a distance of some two hundred yards, to the home of Miss Kate McDaniel. The new family had recently rented her garage apartment. More than a neighbor, Miss Kate taught the fifth through eighth grades in the Home's school.

We had been there a short time when Mr. Acree, returning from his trip, drove by Miss Kate's house. Busy talking, we didn't see him until he had stopped the truck and backed into the driveway. He stepped from the cab and called us; we knew we were in trouble. Mr. Acree removed his belt and began to lash me. During the confusion, Fred dashed off for home fast as his feet allowed. The boss yelled for him to stop, but Fred paid no attention and ran even faster.

Mr. Acree popped me a few blows and told me to hop in the back of the truck. He then charged after Fred, holding his belt with one hand and supporting his trousers with the other. Fred ran faster.

Unsuccessful in the chase, Mr. Acree returned and started the pickup. We roared pass Fred as he topped a small rise in the road. The boss yelled at Fred to stop, but he kept running. In a series of starts and stops that jerked me back and forward, Mr. Acree grew more and more irritated.

He jumped out of the vehicle and again chased after Fred on foot. I mentally cheered for Fred to run faster — run faster. Finally, too winded to continue, the boss ended the chase. His face flushed red with anger as he returned to the pickup, its motor still running. I beamed and thought, 'That's good; he didn't catch Fred.' I turned and looked the other way when he approached the truck; I wanted to conceal the smile on my face. If he had seen my pleasure at the turn of events, he would have walloped me again. I took no chances.

We arrived at the main building about the same time as Fred. Mr. Acree gave him the belt treatment, all the while beaming as if he enjoyed the sweet revenge. He then locked us in the broom closet.

After the long confinement behind the bolted door, we welcomed the supper bell. The fading sounds told us that the girls had marched into the dining hall — the boys would have entered through the front door at the same time. Everyone stood quietly behind an assigned chair and waited for the next bell before setting down. Mr. Acree must have looked over the crowd and noted that we were missing. Apparently, he had forgotten that we were in the closet. He issued orders to release us.

With our heads sheepishly bowed, Fred and I entered the dining room by way of the girls' entrance and shuffled across the floor toward our table. Meanwhile, Mr. Acree explained to the group why he had delayed supper, saying

"The Foster boys are learning that they must get permission before leaving the grounds." Every eye focused on us. We had entered through the girls' door, and this gave us another type problem. Our peers at the table picked up where the boss had stopped.

"Why did you two sissies come in through the girls' entrance? How did you like being in jail?" The teasing and fussing about the delayed supper continued the entire meal, as we suffered through the scorn and taunts by our table mates.

Meanwhile, I felt nothing but contempt for the man at the head table who had submerged Fred and me in this deluge of attention. Mr. Acree served as the Home's superintendent during my first ten years at the orphanage. He totally dominated my life, as well as the lives of the other children. The trouble-filled conflict between us lasted until he left in 1942.

The tension between Mr. Acree and our family started soon after we arrived in 1932. Our mother planned to live with us at the Home, so she asked Mr. Acree to assign her quarters that she might share with her four children. She hoped to keep the family together as a unit, but he refused her request. Without changing the way he ran the place there was no way for him to grant Mother's wish. The children lived in the nursery or dorm, based on age and gender. Mr. Acree required the mothers of the children to act as matrons to the older girls.

Our mother refused to back down from what she viewed as a simple request, and Mr. Acree bristled. Thanks to their headstrong natures, neither he nor she looked for the middle ground. Mother could not live there, given the conflict.

The seeds of bitterness sowed in the wake of Mother's departure sprouted, grew and yielded a crop of problems. The impasse led to ten years of conflict, as long as Mr. Acree held the job. He displayed a warped bias toward our family and spewed his wrath on us, while playing favorites with certain other children. The members of our family suffered, but there was one exception.

From the time both girls were six years old, my sister Barbara became friends with Sara Acree, the boss's daughter. They played together daily. The friendship proved Barbara's good fortune; at times, she sat at the Superintendent's dinner table with Sara. No other child enjoyed such status. Barbara, noting that this special treatment came only because the two girls were close, broke off the friendship.

The bias shown by Mr. Acree toward my older sister, June, more closely mirrored that which Fred and I endured. One evening, several teenage girls waited in the hall near Acree's living quarters. They engaged in lively talk before beginning the nightly study hall. Suddenly the boss appeared at the hall door and said,

"You girls stop making all that racket."

A few more girls arrived and continued the vibrant and jovial mood, without having heard the warning. Mr. Acree again appeared at the door, but this time he was in a bad mood. Glancing around for the nearest object that might help him vent his wrath, he spied the rung from a broken chair. He picked up the weapon and headed for one girl — June. He whacked her leg several times, bringing blood. She still carries the scars.

Another event will attest to his malice toward her. One morning before driving the bus to high school, Mr. Acree called a group of girls into his office. June's friend suffered from cramps, and had not dressed for school.

"Why aren't you ready for school?" He asked the girl.

"I feel too sick to go to school."

Mr. Acree snapped at the girl, "You're not sick; go get yourself ready and get on the bus, you're going to school."

Without pausing to think how the boss might react, June blurted, "She is sick, she's been sick since we got up this morning."

Mr. Acree turned away from the ill girl and focused on June. He slapped her across the face with his open palm, saying,

"There, that'll teach you to sass me."

By confirming her friend's illness, June had become the target. Even with the truth on her side, a girl must never show disrespect by questioning the boss's decision. Members of our family were often the targets when he vented his fury. On many occasions, I saw the ice-cold stares, heard the caustic words and felt the pain of his anger.

Besides looking for reasons to punish me, Mr. Acree seemed to enjoy shocking me into a state of terror. More than once, when he prepared to flog me, he pulled his pearl-handle knife from his pocket and said,

"Go to that tree over there and cut me a switch."

Walking toward the tree, I debated with myself about the switch's size. A large branch would cause great pain and leave those painful red welts. If I brought a small cutting, Mr. Acree would tell me to lift the back of my shirt and roll my trousers above my knees. A small switch applied directly to the skin yielded a terrible sting. I usually picked a medium one, hopeful that it was big enough that he would not tell me to bare my skin.

From the first few months of our arrival in 1932, and lasting for ten long years, Mr. Acree was my doom at every turn. Even with my best efforts, I failed to please him. On the slightest pretense, he found reason to lay belt or switch marks on my backside. Even with his open hostility a spiritual factor seemed to protect me. Of course, I tried to avoid the whippings, but our conflict ran deeper than simple punishment.

A major item of Mr. Acree's management style was to raise the child's anxiety level. The tactic worked quite well for him, so he used it extensively. For some reason, it didn't seem to work on me from age eleven. My refusal to cower — that I showed a lack of fear — he had to notice. The other boys sensed this strange link between us. When they needed his permission, for whatever reason, they asked me to make the request. For example;

"Mr. Acree, may we ride to town with you?"

"Mr. Acree, may we go to Garretts?"

Or during that first warm day of April, I asked,

"May we shed our shoes and go barefoot for the summer?"

The boss often used these or other occasions of a chance meeting to assign extra work, so I tried to stay out of his sight. Still, when we needed to ask him for permission, I did the asking. He had not broken my spirit, though at times that seemed to be his main goal.

The first job he gave me at age six, the one that required that I keep the front lawn clean, offered him many excuses to flog me. No matter what the time of day, if he found trash or paper on my area of the lawn, I stood a good chance of receiving a flogging. It's impossible to count the number of times Mr. Acree used this sham to thrash me. Two such cases, even though they took place more than half a century ago, remain fresh in my mind.

One day, when about nine years old, I looked out the window of the boy's building and saw Mr. Acree approaching. He did not see me on the second floor. He often sported a swagger stick under his arm; this day, he carried a three-foot long piece of fishing cane. Suddenly he pulled a piece of gum from his pocket, unwrapped and popped it in his mouth and then threw the wrapper on my grass. I guessed his next move. The moment he entered the door he yelled for me to come downstairs.

When I reached the bottom of the steps he grabbed me by the ear, saying

"Let's go."

Out the front door and down the porch steps we marched. Using my ear as an improvised leash, Mr. Acree pulled me along the sidewalk until we reached the same gum wrapper he had dropped a few moments earlier.

The thrashing wasn't eventful except that it was the first time he used a doctored cane pole on me. He had cut several long splits in it, leaving many edges as sharp as razors. Perhaps he was trying out his new weapon; it did make for a more painful whipping. Even the heavy overalls I wore failed to protect me from the torture. The welts lasted several days. Had today's views toward child abuse prevailed in the thirties, the red stripes on my backside would have brought him to court and removed him as superintendent of the orphanage.

That round was the worst whipping I received at his hand. I here refer to physical hurt. Another event, however, brought me greater anguish than did the pain from the split cane. It happened about a year later when I was ten, and as on former occasions, the lawn chore was the source of trouble.

With the high school girls on board, Mr. Acree stopped the bus at our building to pick up the boys. The boss spied a brown bag and other trash on my lawn as they boarded the bus. He stepped off the bus and shouted for me to come out where he stood. Every eye on the bus focused on me when I walked toward the boss.

"Pick up that trash," he demanded, pointing to a brown paper bag and waxed paper. He removed his belt.

Drop the trash here at my feet.

I walked on the grass toward the trash to obey his order. A heavy dew had settled that cool morning.

"Down on your hands and knees," he said, "I want you to crawl across the lawn, pick up the trash with your teeth and drop it here," and pointed to his feet.

Dropping to my knees, I crawled across the dew-soaked grass, picked up the litter in my teeth and delivered it to his feet exactly as instructed. He then gave me a few whacks with his belt, but the real punishment included the total scene.

I can tap into my feelings of that moment, some five-plus decades ago. I can still feel the pain of his belt on my back. I can still sense my wet hands and knees in the cold grass. I can still taste the limp paper bag and wax paper dangling from my mouth. I can still see the astonished faces of the bus load of high school students.

This ugly affair remains the deepest humiliation that I have ever known. Nothing else comes close to this vivid memory of the bad feelings I hold about the man.

It's little wonder that I rejoiced at the news that day in 1942. The day I learned that Superintendent Acree was to leave the orphanage. Just as most Americans born before 1930 can recall the Japanese attack on Pearl Harbor, I hold Mr. Acree's exit with the same strength in my recall. I know the exact location, and what I was doing, the moment I heard the good news. We had received a carload of coal. Much of the load had spilled outside the bin when the driver dumped it. The boss had told me to shovel the overflow back into the bin.

When I heard the news, I could scarcely believe that this man who had been my absolute boss for ten years was about to leave. Although we had no way of knowing it, he had planned to give up the job when he reached the age of fifty. Fortunately, he stayed with the plan.

In spite of the trouble and pain he gave me over a ten-year period, Mr. Acree helped me in many ways. He instilled in me a set of important values, virtues and lessons that have stayed with me. I learned to be punctual, to follow orders and to respect authority. He imbued me with a 'will to work' and taught me that I alone am responsible for my actions. More important than all these lessons, Mr. Acree's guidance has shown that I can survive a deluge of trouble. My learning of these truths has helped to balance the scale between value and pain.

Mr. B. F. Widgery

Mr. Widgery was the first of three other men who would fill the superintendent's office during my last five years at the orphanage. He and his wife, along with their daughter who had just finished high school, arrived in 1942. They came from Memphis where he had held the rank of major in the Salvation Army.

Mr. Widgery was about the same age as Mr. Acree, but there the likeness ended. The new man was shorter and heavier, and thanks to my good fortune, slower to anger. The man projected a gentler, less spiteful image. More than a better attitude, he didn't whip the children.

This change of superintendents helped to improve my outlook toward the orphanage, but I still wished to leave the place. Little did I know just how close Mr. Widgery would come toward helping me fulfill that desire.

One late-spring day when I was fourteen, several of us worked in a field east of the chicken house. Weeds vied with the foot-tall tomato plants in the rock-studded, red clay dirt. We often gathered and hauled away these stones, but more showed up each spring when we plowed the ground.

Mr. Widgery had ordered us to put out an extra large planting of tomatoes. If good weather allowed us to make an average crop, we'd have grown more tomatoes than we needed. He apparently had aimed to bring in a big harvest and convert any surplus into cash.

We fertilized the field with chicken manure, and the tomato plants thrived in the rocky ground. The tomatoes did well, but the weeds grew even faster and nearly choked out the crop. The rocks made our controlling the weeds more difficult.

Mr. Widgery seldom came out to the fields where we worked. He knew little about farming, yet that day he was on hand to watch us hoe the tomatoes. The weeds were almost as tall as the plants under cultivation. At the moment the boss looked my way, my hoe bounced off a buried rock to cut down a tomato plant.

He walked over to me and said in a calm voice,

"Buddy you should cut the weeds, not the tomato plants."

After saying these few words, he turned and left the field. I was unable to explain that he had seen an accident, so I dismissed the matter from my mind.

About ten days later, my mother paid us a surprise visit. We were happy to see her, as she rarely came to the orphanage during those years. The main reason for this visit remained a secret between her and Mr. Widgery. He had expelled me for chopping down tomato plants, and had asked Mother to come and take me away.

Both kept this fact from me at the time — Mother told me the purpose of the trip 25 years later. On the surface, she simply made one of her rare visits.

The boss either forgot the matter or misjudged Mother's resolve. After his letter arrived, she took up the case of my discharge with certain Knoxville lodge members. She brought letters from these contacts, and used them to persuade Mr. Widgery to change his mind. It was years later that Mother told me of her talks with Mr. Widgery; I barely recalled the matter.

If she had given me the facts at the time, I may have done things differently. Had I known that my cutting a few tomato plants might cause my release, the stroke of my hoe would have been willful. I would have welcomed a release from the place, whatever the reason. At fourteen, I still viewed the orphanage as a jail and saw my plight as hopeless.

About this time, I felt that something was wrong in my life — but what? I often lay awake and wondered what was missing. I seethed through the long nights and detested my situation. Thoughts of adventure stirred within me. I felt trapped, as an animal caught in a snare. I was trapped — I craved freedom!

Like an endless melody burning into my head, these passions cried out for relief. Others at the orphanage felt the same way. A couplet, which I often heard, and repeated, gave voice to this frustration. It went:

"One of these days, it won't be long,"
"They'll call my name, and I'll be gone."

Never did I plan to run away — there was no place to go. Boys had tried this a few times, but the superintendent had always found and returned them.

In the wake of this puberty-linked firestorm, I slowly learned to accept my status — to live at peace with myself. About this time I turned to football and studies at high school. This painful phase of my life eased into the past. That bitter feeling at being trapped, at living at the orphanage, slowly faded. Perhaps this change had already begun, but Mr. Widgery's coming seemed to help spawn an improved outlook.

Even though this new boss had little knowledge of how to run a farm, he had a good eye for money matters. From the time he settled in, Mr. Widgery seemed to use this special flair of his. Was it for his personal gain?

He told us to move all the bales of hay from the barn, saying, "Load the wagon as high as possible, for we're sending all the hay to market." Selling the hay was only the start. He later converted many items to cash, including the spare corn and wheat. Many tools, along with the farming equipment, vanished from the place. With fewer people living at the orphanage, a station wagon met our transportation needs; he sold the school bus.

The defense workers at nearby Camp Campbell needed more housing, so Mr. Widgery had us divide the unused school and dorm rooms. We strung wires and draped sheets across them to make four living quarters of each large room. With the added renters, he took in more cash, but we saw few results of it.

Mr. Widgery's tenure lasted almost a year. Rumors made the rounds that the Board of Trustees asked him to leave. This drew little reaction from us; it didn't matter one way or the other. Although his exit, by itself, was not important, the news of his replacement brought me some anxious moments. None other than Mr. Grey Acree was to take charge again. Fortunately, he was only to stay for a short time. I beamed with joy to learn that he would remain until the Trustees could find a replacement. I could live with that.

Mr. Acree had changed during his absence. His former attitude had softened and he now came across as mellowed, more relaxed. Gone, along with some of his former vigor, were the spite and hostility that marked his nature during the earlier stint.

Mr. G. W. Kilpatrick

He was a tower of a man, and lean; Mr. Kilpatrick stood well over six feet tall and stared through black horn-rimmed glasses. Nearly fifty-five years old at the time, he badly needed the job. A friend of his who served on the Home's Board of Trustees landed the appointment for him. The new line of work called for a person who had some mastery of working with children, but Mr. Kilpatrick possessed few skills in this area. Friendship carried more weight than the ability to manage.

This third superintendent arrived during World War II from Copper Hill, Tennessee where he had held a school teacher's job. In spite of his academic background, Mr. Kilpatrick spoke in a way that seemed strange to us.

People from the eastern section of the state, especially those who lived in the rural mountainous locations, spoke with a distinctive area dialect. His twang and use of slang words, such as "Ain't" and "You'ens," sounded odd to people in Middle Tennessee.

He'd say, for example, "You'ens boys go rake the leaves."

Picking up on this strange word usage, we made fun of him. Beyond his earshot, we would say, "We'ns will rake them'ens leaves."

Miss Frances, our teacher, had lectured us about the use of certain words and good diction. His strange words fell on our ears and, in a strange way, give us a sense of superiority. We had great fun using this leverage on this former school teacher. From the beginning, this feeling of strength allowed us to poke fun at the man. It was a trivial thing; still, we used the matter to our advantage. This, among his other faults, prevented Mr. Kilpatrick from gaining full control over those in his charge. The population had dropped to about two dozen boys and girls upon his arrival.

He walked around with his arms folded across his chest, looking as if he didn't belong. He was out of his element. In one way, his nature differed from the prior superintendents. Where the earlier bosses saw us as things, Mr. Kilpatrick viewed us as rowdy fifth graders whom he had to control, but he couldn't do it.

He faced another problem, a fault he did not overcome. Like Mr. Widgery before him, he was not a farmer. This fact, besides his novel way of talking, hampered his ability to take charge. Just weeks before Mr. Kilpatrick arrived, Mr. Williamson the retired farmer who worked at the orphanage for about a year, left. This added to the boss's problem, but the leave taking made an opening for Dewey James to become the new farm boss.

Dewey was no stranger to us — he grew up at the Home. The Army discharged him because of a line-of-duty injury he received. After serving his country, Dewey came back home.

He filled the job of farm boss very well, but soon a problem developed. His ideas about discipline convinced us that he had forgotten what life at the orphanage was like. Dewey's hard driving, but non-violent, methods of dealing with the boys stemmed from two major sources — discipline learned from his recent Army career and from life under Mr. E.E. York and Mr. Acree. Mr. York was superintendent until 1927 when Mr. Acree took over. This was five years before our family arrived.

Even with the strict discipline Dewey brought to the job as farm boss, Mr. Kilpatrick failed to control the boys. Instead, his tenure slowly declined to a state of near chaos. One day Mr. Kilpatrick told seven of us to go help a nearby farmer harvest his hay. The neighbor had cut and raked the crop, but needed our help to bail and haul it to his barn.

We headed toward the neighbor's farm, but began to question the project as we walked. This was the first time the boss had told us to work for someone else, but had not explained why he gave us the job. The neighbor had not helped us. After thinking about the situation, and since there had been no talk of pay, we decided to ignore the boss's order. We reasoned — no wage, no work.

Instead of showing up at the neighbor's hayfield we headed for the Red River, our favorite spot for fun on a warm summer day, the swimming hole. After a morning of skinny dipping in the muddy river, we arrived in time for dinner, or the mid-day meal.

Mr. Kilpatrick knew earlier in the day that we had not shown up at the neighbor's, but he had no idea of where we spent the morning. After the meal, the boss ordered all seven boys to his office, a large room behind the parlor of the main building.

He seated himself behind the big desk near a corner and we stood in a curved row before him. I held the center spot in the stair-step line, with three smaller boys to my right and three larger to my left. For what seemed like several minutes, the man glared at us through his dark-rimmed glasses without saying a word. We stood in silence before him, our eyes on the carpet.

Finally, he began, "You boys must obey my orders."

Slowly, he worked himself into a state of agitation, explaining that we must do as he said, because he was in charge. At last he decided to teach each boy in the line a lesson, using his belt as a tool.

Mr. Kilpatrick removed the weapon and headed toward the younger boys to my right. Secretly, I felt good about not having to feel the sting of that first lash. My brother Fred, still the youngest boy, became his first target — a moving target.

Fred darted behind the line of boys as the boss lifted his arm to strike the first blow. He tried to grab Fred, but too late. A roar of nervous laughter filled the room as Fred zipped behind the line and toward the desk, with Mr. Kilpatrick running after him. They circled the desk twice, but the gap between them held. On the third round, Fred popped out the opened office door and sped down the hall toward the front entry, the boss trailing.

Gasping for air after his futile pursuit, Mr. Kilpatrick returned to the office and plopped down in his chair. With a bowing head, he gazed at our feet for several moments. Finally, without looking up, the boss waved a hand, and said,

"You'ens are dismissed."

Thanks to Fred's speed, seven boys avoided the belt that day. This victory raised our spirits and led to more acts of open defiance. At the usual six o'clock wake-up time one morning, the alarm clock opened the day with its loud clang. Disturbed by the noise, a boy yelled

"I'm not ready to get up yet" and threw the timepiece out an open second story window.

The clock continued its alarm, although it had landed on a concrete sidewalk some twenty feet below the window. Each of the twelve boys in the room decided to stay in bed.

Dewey exploded with anger when he walked in the dorm at seven-thirty and found us still in bed. Enraged by our pretense at being asleep, he overturned every occupied bed in the room. We slowly lifted ourselves from the floor and went about our usual business, but it wasn't over yet.

The indignity we suffered at being turned out of bed annoyed us. Refusing either to clean the room or straighten the upset beds, we slept on the mattresses lying on the floor. This lasted until Mr. Western Grizzard, a local Board of Trustees member, had inspected the mess in our dorm. He was sympathetic with our point of view and said he'd take action.

About this time, we decided to play a trick on Mr. Kilpatrick. We rang the door bell at the main building, and drew back into the dark night. When he opened the front door we peppered the porch with rocks. He refused to answer the bell after the second ring.

Later the same night we rolled a fifty-five-gallon barrel to the middle of the baseball diamond and beat on it with sticks as if pounding a drum. Armed with a long flashlight, Mr. Kilpatrick walked out the back door to investigate the noise. Lumps of coal, incoming from the furnace area, landed at his feet and forced his retreat. A few minutes later, the boss sped off in the station wagon toward Dewey's house, less than a half mile away. We heard nothing more from him that night.

Soon after this incident, Mr. Kilpatrick took to a sick bed. Apparently, the stresses of the job had gotten to him and made it hopeless for him to go on. Our defiant acts, plus the break in his health, helped him arrive at a basic decision. Two days later, an ambulance arrived at the orphanage and drove away with Mr. Kilpatrick. We didn't learn the exact nature of his illness.

It was time for us to break in a new boss.

Mr. A. S. Byrom

They wore invisible wings. Mr. and Mrs. Byrom didn't look the part, but they were angels. His age, the graying hair and his slight hunch suggested that Mr. Byrom had known a long and strenuous life. Although he was in his mid sixties at the time, it failed to disqualify Mr. Byrom for the job of superintendent.

> They wore invisible wings. Mr. and Mrs. Byrom didnt look the part, but they were angels.

He brought a new style of running the orphanage; Mr. and Mrs. Byrom assumed the roles of surrogate parents to all the children. This took some time to get accustomed to. As an abused dog warms slowly to a new, but kinder, master — so were my feelings toward this new boss.

From the beginning, they treated everyone the same — this included the children as well as the old folks under their care. They saw each human as deserving a full measure of respect. Was this latest change for real? Would it last? Yes, it did.

The ease by which this gentle man dealt with people made it hard for one to guess his former background. He had farmed a small plot of land in Middle Tennessee, and his wife had been at his side. Both were friendly and understanding. They had personalities that well suited them for their new jobs — a perfect team.

I was sixteen in 1944, the year that Mr. Byrom brought to the orphanage this fresh new policy. It was a welcome break with the past. He took a personal interest in each boy and girl. Instead of barking orders at us, he suggested or simply advised a course of action. Before long, the Byroms had earned my total respect.

During his tenure the children enjoyed a burst of new freedoms. He allowed the high school girls to go out on dates and inspired each person to attend a local church of choice — without an escort. We were to take an active role in the events at school. He allowed us to invite friends from outside. All of this helped to boost our social, scholastic and spiritual lives.

By the time Mr. Byrom arrived, my school activities, mainly football, had moved to the top spot in my mind. Unlike the former bosses, he did not object if a school project happened to outrank the farm work.

He saw that each boy and girl received a weekly allowance, a first at the Home. This enabled us to stand tall when mixing with the other high school students. As a teenager, I had longed for this boost to my self-respect. Mr. Byrom's changes did just that. Although the allowance was small, it filled a basic need. My self image soared. Superintendent Byrom affected the lives of all the children in the same way.

In 1945, a few months before my sister June graduated from high school, she met and fell in love with Carl Mann, a neighbor boy. He had joined the Navy. Carl arranged a few days leave to attend June's graduation, after which they planned to marry. Mr. and Mrs. Byrom showed an interest in the romance and helped make their plans go smoothly. He bought June a bridal gown, surprised her with a small dowry and, as a stand-in father, gave her away at the ceremony.

After a brief wedding trip, Carl returned to the war and June left the orphanage to live with his parents. Mr. Byrom had made June an offer; she could stay at the Home and attend Austin Peay College in Clarksville. Instead, she took a war-time job as a time-keeper in a local plant where they made gas masks. She worked for Mode Hampton, a man who had grown up at the Home two decades earlier.

I graduated high school in 1947, two years after June's class. Barbara still had another year to go and Fred, three years. Even so, we all three left the orphanage at the same time. Fred would live with our grandmother in Knox County and go to Young High, the same Knoxville high school that Mother had attended.

Barbara wanted to leave, but she also wanted to stay and complete her 1948 senior year at Clarksville with her classmates. Mr. Byrom suggested that she return after spending the summer in Knoxville. Barbara agreed to this plan. She had a special classmate in mind — Mack Johnson. He lived near the orphanage. They had dated for some time and would marry less that a year after finishing high school.

During my final three years at the Home, the Byroms flooded me with an endless deluge of friendship and acted as stand-in parents. They filled my need for approval. This support helped me when I needed it the most — as I prepared to leave the orphanage.

Mr. Byrom endowed me with a super legacy. He built my self-confidence and assured me that my only limits were those that I put upon myself. I accepted his wonderful gifts and brought them with me beyond the moment that I had longed for — my release from the orphanage.

While doing research for this book, I had access to the official record books of the Odd Fellows Home. Each former resident had a personalized page in the large book. It registered the entry and departure dates along with other data. Few of these records carried extra comments by the superintendents, but Mr. Byrom had penned at the bottom of my page the following note:

"Left the Home May 19, 1947, finishing high school with all honors May 1947. He was an exceptionally good and honest boy. This boy is appreciative, a deep thinker, studied hard and retained. He was a natural mechanic, could do so many things to help the Home. He entered the University of Tennessee and is taking an engineering course. He was kind and obedient. I am proud of him, for he was a real Buddy to all."

Chapter 6

World War II

The World War II brought many changes to our lives at the orphanage. Some were major and others of less substance. The greatest had to do with the call to arms and the orphanage's waning numbers.

From 1928 to 1935 the Home's population of children and old folks grew larger. It put a strain on the facilities. When my family arrived in 1932, nearly two hundred people lived at the orphanage. In the late 1930's, however, this trend had begun to fade. A better business climate across the state and country helped to slow the pace of new arrivals. The numbers peaked before the war started in 1941. Fewer than two dozen remained by the time I left in 1947. This fact led to changes in the way we used the living quarters.

Fewer old folks sought refuge because not as many needed a helping hand. In the span of a few years the old folks' and orphans' needs began to lessen in concert with the sunny business climate. The war was but one factor that drove this trend. With the hard times easing, families were better able to manage their affairs without help from the Odd Fellows.

This turn for the better seemed to help one and all. In the late thirties and early forties, some new laws brought more aid. Among the public acts were the new Social Security program and Aid to Families with Dependent Children. The war-time economy did help to ease the tough times. Even without its wage earner, the family found it more easy to survive.

Fewer boys and girls came to the orphanage; the young people living there grew up and left and the old folks died. We moved from the boys' building in 1939 when Mr. Acree rented the former school and living quarters to the Tennessee State Highway Patrol. Their training class lasted for several weeks before they moved out.

The fifteen or so boys who remained moved to a large room above the dining hall. That space that had served as a dorm for the young girls. They moved in with the older girls directly above the kitchen. With this change, we needed to build a stairwell from the outside near the dining hall's front door.

Though this shift in our living space had started months before, the building of Camp Campbell would bring a sea of changes to the area. Only a few miles away, the mammoth job began in 1942. This large training camp for airborne troops would stretch along the state line of Kentucky and Tennessee. Thousands of workers swarmed in to help build this new army base.

The onrush became a major problem as it raised the demand for living space way beyond the supply. The locals rented their garages, and in a few cases, their chicken houses to the workers. Meanwhile, there were fewer new children and old folks left at the Home. We turned the surplus space into living units and rented to the workers.

Mr. B.F. Widgery, who came after Mr. Acree, entered the landlord business on a grand scale. He opened more space to this influx of workers by moving the old folks to the main building and changing their rooms into rental units.

We sectioned off the two school rooms by hooking blankets on the clothes-lines strung from wall to wall. Each of the former classrooms turned into four rental units.

All types of people sought housing with us. A family with several small children moved in. One of their daughters, a small six-year-old who wore her blond curls in the Shirley Temple style, died suddenly soon after they arrived. The parents claimed that her death was due to something she ate or drank.

The small casket lay in the parlor. I, a teenager, looked down at the motionless girl and thought, "How sad." She would never know the pleasure of growing to adulthood. My heart suffered in a scene that depressed everyone. The family moved away soon after the funeral, but the image of a beautiful child asleep in the small coffin remained with me.

Without an autopsy, the cause of death remained a mystery. Many rumors passed around. One theory claimed that the parents offered candy to each of their four children, but that they had laced one piece with poison. The insurance money, according to the gossip mill, was the reason the child died.

The child's death brought our water supply under suspicion. Specialists from Camp Campbell came to run some tests. They found nothing major, but ruled that the problem might be the lack of chlorine in the water. They suggested that we closely monitor the pump and flow of chlorine. This job fell to me after each day at high school. For weeks afterward, I jogged a mile to Garretts, the point of our water supply, and checked the system.

One of the families that rented from us will always remain in my recall. The father often came home in a state of drunkenness. The windows were open about eleven o'clock one summer evening when this man returned to his apartment. He began to beat his children. The screams floated through the warm night air to where I slept in the main building, less than 150 feet away.

Their mother shrieked each time a child cried out with pain. As she tried to protect the little ones from the man's drunken rage, she became the object of his attack. The cries of defenseless people, magnified through the still night air, told me they suffered extreme physical pain.

The young voices pleading for help touched me deeply. Although I thought of going to their rescue, the fear for my own safety kept me from getting involved. Later, when recalling the piercing cries of the little ones, I regretted that I had lacked the courage to help them. Besides the remorse and shame I felt, I wondered why a father would so cruelly treat his own helpless children. The screams of those young ones haunted me long after the family moved away.

A few children from the nearby neighborhood attended our grade school after we had moved to the main building. Myrtle Marshall and Junior Binion lived on adjoining farms. Myrtle, along with Mary Frances Williams and me from the orphanage, made up the fifth grade. Only three people were in the third grade — Junior, plus my sister Barbara and Ben Davidson of the Home.

Junior's father sharecropped and raised hogs on the farm to our north. Some two hundred pigs roamed the hills. The owner had contracted with Camp Campbell to receive their edible garbage. Twice each day, an olive drab truck arrived from the army base, moved to the hillside and scattered the food scraps over the fields.

The truck driver unloaded each batch at a different spot. The hogs looked forward to the feast and lined up behind the garbage truck to eat their way across the field. Within an hour nothing remained but a line of corn cobs, melon rinds and grapefruit skins scattered along the hillside. The hogs thrived on the scraps of army leftovers.

Early one summer morning fifteen men arrived at Mr. Binion's pig field in an olive-drab bus. The army vehicle stopped under a shade tree at our common fence and they stepped from the bus. Curious about the visit, we had walked to our corn field near where the bus stopped. All the men wore light gray uniforms except for two army guards.

The two soldiers who carried rifles draped over their arms ordered the others to climb the fence into our cornfield. Once across the fence, some men began to remove their shirts, each of which carried the letters POW on the back. A few wore olive drab undershirts, some wore white T-shirts and others wore no shirt at all. These men were German prisoners of war from Camp Campbell.

A guard called for their attention. With his rifle slung across his shoulder, he showed them how to use a hoe by chopping a few weeds from the corn. After learning the basics, each prisoner began to chop weeds in the field of one-foot-tall corn.

Uneasy with fear and doubt, we watched from a distance as the prisoners of war worked our field. One guard sat under a shade tree near the fence and another moved with the row of Germans. They hoed one row of corn and about half of the second. All of a sudden, a POW in the line dropped his hoe, yelled and raced toward the fence. The other prisoners dropped their hoes and followed. Surprised, both guards whipped their rifles to the ready position.

> The guards soon lowered their weapons, for their German prisoners had not tried to escape.

"Swine, swine," yelled the Germans as they raced across the corn field. They yelled other strange words. The military guards soon lowered their weapons, for their prisoners had not tried to escape. The excitement came about because the pigs were helping themselves to the visitors' lunch. Their food, packed in five-gallon lard cans, rested under the shade tree by the fence. The pigs mistook the olive drab bus for the truck that brought them the army's eatable garbage. The metal cans offered little protection against the pack of hungry hogs.

Our Nation's war policy allowed captured Germans to do farm work. Each POW was to receive payment of eighty cents per day. I didn't learn whether the farmer or the government paid this wage. The group of war prisoners returned the next day to finish hoeing our cornfield, and we didn't see them again.

During the war, new victory gardens sprang up in many back lawns, but not in ours at the orphanage. Gardening wasn't new to us. Before the war began, we at the orphanage already grew vegetables and fruits for canning or preserving. This allowed us to enjoy them long after the end of the normal growing season.

The tomatoes ripened in mid July and lasted until cool weather, but we often ate them as late as Thanksgiving Day. We stripped the green fruit from the vines just before the season's first frost, wrapped them in brown paper and squirreled them away. We also saved fresh onions, apples and potatoes, but we stored these items in bins without wrapping them.

During the war years, the food producers served a vital need, so the war planners urged farmers to grow as much food as possible. In exchange, the country deferred from military service the young men who worked on a farm. When the war started I was thirteen. I felt a deep sense of pride — I helped to grow food and raised beef cattle and hogs. The war did not change this function at the orphanage.

During the war, we observe a "Meatless Tuesday." The local ration boards issued coupon books based on the number in a household. There were stamps for meat, canned goods, and other scarce food staples. The grocers collected these stamps as they sold the rationed items. Sugar, tea and meat were especially scarce. We at the orphanage received more coupons than we needed and took pride in the fact that we seldom used all our ration stamps.

Some non-food items were scarce during the mid forties. A shortage of rubber latex made auto tires hard to come by. Nothing equaled, or even come close, to pure rubber for use in making tires. The latex came from trees of the South Pacific, an area under enemy control. Tire makers looked for a stand-in for rubber, but failed to find a substance until nearly the end of the war.

The government, in trying to make the tires last longer, set a speed limit on open highway driving. It was thirty-five miles per hour. Anyone who needed a new tire applied to the ration board. Unless an applicant could prove a tie-in to the war effort, the board turned down the request. Because we lived on a farm we could buy all the tires the needed.

After Pearl Harbor, the auto builders shifted to war items instead of bringing out new models each year. The older clinkers required frequent care to keep them up and running. In spite of the difficulty in finding repair parts, we managed to keep the trucks and farm machines in a state of good repair. Instead of calling for help from the outside, we patched the ailing machines, fixed the broken water pipes and repaired the bad electric circuits.

Mr. Byrom owned an old Plymouth, but its worn-our motor would not start. I asked him to let me fix the car, providing we found the needed parts. He located the items and gave me the go-ahead. I worked on the sedan for almost three days, replacing the piston rings and crank shaft bearings without pulling the engine from the chassis. The newly overhauled car surprised both Mr. Byrom and me when it sputtered back to life the first time we tried to start it.

The country's war effort suffered from a shortage of gasoline. Each car or truck carried a ration decal on its windshield. These stickers from the ration board came in three classes of fuel usage. An "A" sticker meant the owner drove a short way to a job, but had no direct link with the war effort. Anyone who held a defense job, or lived a long distance from work and needed more gas, received a class "B" label. The ration board issued "C" stickers for those vehicles used full time in the war effort. All farmers fell in this last group, so both, our farm truck and the pickup, carried "C" decals.

Everyone did his part in saving gas. A popular saying went, "Is this trip really necessary?" At age sixteen I worked at a job after school and Saturdays, one that helped me see, first-hand, the effects of the gas shortage.

In 1944, Mr. Western Grizzard, a Board of Trustee member who lived in nearby Clarksville, hired me to work at his filling station. It stood one block from College Street near downtown. He taught me to meet every car before it came to a stop at his Red Ace gas station. I followed this and his other orders — to pump the gasoline only after the driver had handed over the ration stamps. I pasted the gas stamps on the blank sheets of a booklet furnished for the purpose. Each week, we mailed the stamp-filled pages to the ration board.

One morning, a man driving a car with an "A" sticker on the windshield's lower right side pulled into the station. I met him at the pump.

"Fill'er up," said the driver.

He presented more than enough stamps to cover a tank of gas. After pumping the gasoline, cleaning the windshield and checking the pressure of each tire I said, "Want me to check the oil?"

"No thanks, I'm in a hurry."

He slipped me a five-dollar bill and said, "Keep the change."

The amount on the pump came to $4.63, which meant that he'd given me a 37 cent tip. What a surprise! No customer had never tipped me for doing my job. I then noted that the man had given me a variety of ration stamp. They were of each type — A's, B's and C's. This, and the strange tip, led me to believe that something was wrong. I took down his tag number as he sped away and then phoned my boss.

"Mr. Grizzard, a customer just gave me three different types of gas stamps and was in a big rush after I filled his tank. I wanted to call you before I pasted the different stamps in the pad. He gave me a tip and then sped away, so I wrote down his license number."

"What's the number?"

I told him.

"Don't do anything until I call you back."

Before the next customer drove in, Mr. Grizzard phoned.

"The police will be over there shortly." He explained. "This morning, someone on the other side of town robbed a filling station and stole some loose gas stamps."

I gave the police a description of the driver and car that carried a Stewart County tag. I heard nothing more about the matter, and don't know if the police made an arrest.

My work at the gas station lasted only a few weeks, for spring football was at hand. I wanted to go straight to the practice field after school. Pumping gas was less important than my making the football team. The Clarksville High School sports program continued through the war years.

Although we still played football, the nation needed help, and its war effort called for the public to make changes. The war effort took precedence over one's other needs. Support surged with the bombing of Pearl Harbor and reached a crest after many boys had marched off to war. It seemed that each citizen stood behind the nation and its goal of total victory. Before Pearl Harbor, however, the sentiment was different.

In 1940 and 1941, before the country went to war, the Selective Service System had called up several of our alumni. The term of their army duty was to run for a year. By mid-1941, a few of these drafted boys came back for a visit. They told us that a new motto was making the rounds at the army base. It was "OHIO," an acronym for "Over The Hill In October." These soldiers planned to leave the service at the end of the one-year call, even though the street gossip said the Army would extend the term from one to two years.

The draftees' critical mind-set faded after the Pearl Harbor attack. One of our alumni lived through the event at Scholfield Barracks. Congress did change the terms of service for these early draftees. Instead of adding a year, they were in "For the duration." Their first duty was to defeat the enemy.

It seemed that the entire media worked to shape the public's mind; nothing short of a total victory would do. The movies, papers and radio programs helped sell war bonds. Even Tom and Jerry of the cartoons joined in the patriot's chorus. I, and many others, put aside our dimes to buy savings stamps, and after they piled up, bought a $25 victory bond. Our proximity to the Camp Campbell army base brought the war close to home.

One morning the heavy traffic's roar drifted toward us from the highway. It lasted for a long time — something big was happening. Ben Davidson and I walked down to Highway 41W to check it out. The volume increased as we drew near the road — the noise came from an endless string of military trucks. They streamed down the hillside and crossed the Red River bridge.

A few cars lined up at the side road. Their drivers wanted to move onto the highway, but found few chances of breaking into the convoy. The military drivers held a short space between the trucks, leaving no room for other traffic. This was the largest concentration of trucks that we had ever seen.

Olive drab jeeps, plus large and small trucks of every class, traveled the southbound lane. An infrequent gap allowed a car or civilian truck to wedge into the steam. The procession lasted into the night. Two small beams of light coming from slits, in the place of glaring headlights, struck the road. These subdued lights reduced the chance of being sighted from the air, once the troops reached the war zone.

At the time we didn't know it, but we saw the 101st Airborne Division on the way to earn their place in the nation's history. The unit left Camp Campbell and headed for a vital role in Europe. The soldiers in the convoy were part of the Allies' strike across the English Channel, and would become America's legendary heroes. Many of them lost their lives fighting the Battle of the Bulge near Bastogne, Belgium.

The people of New Providence, a nearby district, answered the call to support the war effort. They started a civilian defense plan at a school meeting. The asked me, at age fourteen, to became a junior warden. My job, upon hearing the air-raid siren, was to dash a quarter mile to the highway and pull the power switch for the two billboards. People were to turn off all house lights.

One day the chief marshal advised us that he soon planned to hold a practice drill. Later that evening after nightfall, a large siren mounted on a pole near the orphanage screeched a long series of short blasts. I raced to my assigned station, pulled the switches and cast the area into pitch darkness. Neither moon nor stars lit the night sky. Some thirty minutes later, a long blast of the siren gave the all-clear signal.

Before the United States entered the war, the numbers of boys and girls at the orphanage began to lessen. A few of our alumni had either entered the service or answered a draft call before Pearl

Harbor. Life at the orphanage had equipped them for the hardships they would meet in basic training.

They knew how to take orders from superiors and had lived lives that hardened them. This put them ahead of many draftees who were away from a soft home-life for the first time. The new soldiers from the city faced a strong cultural shock. Our boys, toughened by the hard life they lived, easily slid into the army's way of doing things. In this case, Mr. Acree's management style had worked in the nation's best interest.

Nearly three dozen from our big family went into the service. Several of these de facto brothers gave their lives. They were James Bryant, Carl Edwards, J. T. Gurley, Howard (Smiley) Johnson, Eddy Moore and Lewis Smith. Thanks to these, we who remained can still enjoy the God-given, but man defended, blessings of freedom. We viewed all those who served as heroes.

I was eighteen the year the United States won the war. The local draft board ordered me to report for a physical exam on my birthday. The doctor said I was fit for service and board gave me a classification of 1-A. They sent all the qualified new draftees a letter that opened with a friendly, "Greetings." The war was almost over, but I needed only two more months to complete the 3rd year of high school. The board allowed me to remain in school until the term ended.

By May of 1945, the Allied Forces had won a victory in Europe. This assured an almost certain successful end to the war. Our Army Air Corps took the action direct to Japan when it bombed Tokyo. Three months later the United States dealt Japan a knockout blow; it dropped the world's first atomic bombs on Hiroshima and Nagasaki. I had expected the draft board to send me a "Greetings" most any day during the last three months of the war.

The headline of the Clarksville Leaf-Chronicle newspaper read: "Truman Says Atomic Bomb Dropped on Japan." The biggest and best-kept secret of the age was out. I wondered, "What is this atomic bomb?" It opened the atomic age and turned the tide of history. The big event brought the Pacific war to an abrupt end. After the bombs fell, it was no longer necessary to invade Japan with American foot troops. Clearly, this affected me, as my call to arms never came.

The mushroom clouds that rose above Japan not only ended the war they also saved many American lives. Perhaps mine too.

.

Chapter 7
Old Folks

The term, "Senior citizen" found its way into our language around 1950; before that, we used the words "Old folks" when talking about older people. In spite of how it might sound today, we youngsters called the mature men and their wives, or widows, who lived at the home, "Old folks." We meant no offense. Young people then showed a great respect for those who had lived to an advanced age. We answered, "Yes sir," or "Yes ma'am," when an adult's question called for a positive reply.

To us, the children in the orphanage, our elders were a source of knowledge and wisdom. They had tasted the flavors and enjoyed the fruits that came with the gray hair and long lifetime. They were wise in both the good and bad morsels that life had offered. I savored these things with keen anticipation. Like the other children, I gave our elders the respect they deserved.

HOME FOR OUR AGED, stated the giant sign mounted on the old folks' building. A set of outside stairs rose to an upper porch supported by four wooden columns. Chimneys at both ends of the two-story front section towered above the roof. Many red brick houses of this style, dating from the early nineteen hundreds, still dot the South today. Several years earlier this structure had served as a hospital for the orphanage.

Until the mid thirties when the old men moved to this former hospital's rear wing, they lived in an old wooden cottage that stood near the baseball diamond. They moved again in 1944, after Mr. Widgery planned to convert the building into rental flats. The elderly women also moved to the main building at the same time. The reduced numbers of old folks and children alike lived in the same building until the orphanage closed.

The aged and needy members of Odd Fellow lodges came from all parts of Tennessee. These men and their wives, or their widows, had no place to live and were unable to earn a living. They came from a variety of lifestyles to spend their last days at the orphanage.

Former miners, farmers or business clerks, these men had worked at many trades. The ladies had been homemakers.

An old person's placement in the Home came only after an okay by his lodge, and his showing that he was in distress. In a few cases both the needy man and his wife entered the place. The Great Depression was a factor that spiked the need for such a rest home. Times were hard for retired people in those days before the Social Security System got its start. The Home's records show that large numbers of new people arrived in the 1930's.

The children of deceased members, and old folks alike, claimed the promise that the order offered. There were never more than 20 older residents at any one time. It's hard to describe these men and women, but a few stood out.

Mr. Arthur W. Pantall, a plump, gray-headed man, had spent most of his life working in an office before coming to the Home. He showed an uncommon flare for kindness and concern for others. When an associate took to a sick bed, he looked after the patient, brought meals to the room and shaved him. When the need arose Mr. Pantall was there to fill it. During one long period, he dressed a man's open cancer sores each day until the patient died.

As I passed through my pre-teen years I viewed his acts with some question, for they struck me as odd. A buzz passed among the young boys — when Mr. Pantall starts to wait on a sick person, we will soon need to dig a grave. All too often, the forecast came true.

> A buzz passed among the young boys — when Mr. Pantall starts to wait on a sick person, we will soon need to dig a grave. All too often, the forecast came true.

One day I happened to be nearby when Mr. Pantall held a mirror to the face of a sick man. He looked for a trace of moisture, but found none. After assuring himself that the patient was dead, he ripped the pillow case into pieces, closed the man's wide-open mouth and tied a strip around his head and chin. He straightened the dead man's legs, fastened the big toes together and fixed the arms together across the chest. Only then, did he pulled the sheet over the man's face.

"Why did you do that?" I asked.

"This will help the funeral director," said Mr. Pantall.

"But why did you tear up the pillow case?"

"Two reasons — No one wants to sleep on a dead man's pillow case and I didn't have any string."

Beyond his many acts of kindness, Mr. Pantall kept us updated on the progress of world War II. Just as today's TV anchorman speaks the news, he read aloud from pages of the *Clarksville Leaf-Chronicle.* From either the porch or the shade of a maple tree, his deep voice roared:

"German 'boom-bers,' and the defense thrown up by the anti-aircraft guns, blackened the sky over London Thursday morning." He sounded a long double-O when he said bombers.

We listened as if spellbound. Thanks to Mr. Pantall's efforts, I, along with the old men, followed the European war from 1939 on.

My younger sister, Barbara, had a special link to Mr. Pantall. While still quite small, Barbara allowed no one to touch her. Even a friendly pat on the head was too much. Mr. Pantall respected her wish. Whenever Barbara came within earshot, he recited a couplet he made up for such occasions. Much to her delight, he'd say,

> "Black-eyed beauty spot,
> Tennessee touch-me-not."

With the passing years, my feelings toward Mr. Pantall began to change — gradually, I took a more favorable view. Through his care-giving efforts, the man seemed to live the true spirit of an Odd Fellow. By the time I reached my teen years, I held him in high regard. By his being ready to help others in need, he taught me a priceless lesson.

Mr. Pantall remained a long-time resident of the Home and still lived there when it closed in 1948. He survived the institution by some eight years and died in a Nashville nursing home at age eighty-nine. His remains rest in the orphanage cemetery. Seldom does a person of Mr. Pantall's genteel and saint-like virtues come along.

Mr. O. D. Ezell, who lived at the old folks' building with Mr. Pantall, was a few years younger. This man came from a different background. With one leg amputated just below the knee, Mr. Ezell walked with crutches when not using his peg leg. He was sixty years old when he arrived, the youngest of the elderly men who lived at the Home.

Mr. Ezell liked to brag. In a mood of self-assurance, he enjoyed telling about living through many close scrapes. Using a boasting tone, he recalled the time he had accidentally run over a twelve-year-old black girl with his car.

According to his tales, the man had worked at many different jobs. He had spent time as a coal miner, as a mechanic on a Mississippi Riverboat engine and as a carnival worker. Most of Ezell's yarns came across as flights of fancy. No item of dialogue stumped him — he knew a little about every topic.

Let me show you my sharp knife.

Using a piece of leather tacked to the armrest of his rocking chair, he honed a pocket knife to a razor's edge. When a youngster happened to walk near him on the porch, Ezell would grab the boy's arm. Holding tightly, he opened the knife and shaved a few hairs from the boy's arm. This confirmed that the blade was sharp. We soon learned to keep our distance.

Most of his stories were yarns aimed at the ears of willing young listeners. We welcomed his tales as a drought-parched field of corn greets a summer shower. I loved to hear about his adventures, even if they were mostly puff.

"How did you lose your leg Mr. Ezell?" I asked him one day.

"I slept with it sticking out from under the cover one cold night, and it froze."

Later, when Fred asked the same question, Ezell had changed the story.

"My foot got caught in the rear paddle of a river boat," he barked, in the new version.

One day Mr. Ezell hobbled toward the main building where Mr. J. R. McQuerter stood near one of the wooden columns. There the sidewalk narrowed to make room for the column, leaving little room for Ezell to pass. Mr. McQuerter, ten years his senior, was busy talking to a matron. Unaware that he blocked the sidewalk, made no effort to move. Able to pass only if he stepped on the grass, Ezell yelled loudly enough to drown out the sounds of playing children:

"Get out of my damn way."

"This is not your sidewalk. I'll stand where I please," replied Mr. McQuerter. He calmly returned to his conversation with Mrs. Williams.

"We'll just see about that," Ezell said and wheeled around on the peg leg.

He hurried back toward the old folks' building. In a few moments he shuffled out of his room onto the porch and down the three steps. Clasping his open pocket knife, he headed straight for McQuerter.

The two men had exchanged words before, but now their conflict was about to explode into violence. Sensing a need to defend himself, McQuerter reached for his knife, flipped open the three-inch blade and stood his ground. With a stern expression and flashing eyes, Ezell struck first. He drew blood with a slash at the older man's left arm, raised as a shield. Stepping forward, McQuerter landed a slashing blow to Ezell's right side.

My sister June, playing nearby with the other children, saw the blood. She screamed, covered her face and turned away as each man hacked at the other. I too, along with several other children, looked on with horror. The fight lasted for only a few moments, as each bloodied man made gashing blows at his opponent.

Someone called Mr. Acree. He and the other men soon stopped the fight, preventing further damage. Both men needed medical care. Mr. Ezell required immediate care as he had received the most sever cuts. Mr. Acree drove him to the Clarksville Hospital. A few minutes later Mr. McQuerter arrived in the farm truck.

The hospital staff had not known about the conflict, so the two men wound up in the same ward. They renewed the verbal duel from their beds and quarreled until the nurses moved one from the room. Each man had sustained flesh wounds and had to stay in the hospital two days.

Although he didn't start the fight, McQuerter suffered the most loss. Mr. Acree consulted with the man's lodge and arranged for him to live with a brother in Arkansas. Mr. Ezell remained — he had no place to go.

For weeks after the fight, Ezell bragged that he was careful to use only slashing blows.

"I could have killed him with a stab," he said, "but I didn't want to face a murder charge."

In spite of this quarrel, the old folks generally led tranquil lives. Hoping only to end the balance of their golden years without worry, the seniors were exempt from farm work or other chores. A few of them were healthy enough and able to walk well enough to do odd jobs. They worked with the children on easy tasks. Mr. J. T. Rinehart, a former carpenter, often practiced his trade as he helped with repairs around the place. At times the women assisted on group projects, such as canning peaches or snapping beans.

Special friendships formed between the old folks and children. Mr. S.R. Lee, the oldest man, took to my brother Fred, who for years was the youngest child at the orphanage. My sister June enjoyed a friendship with Mrs. Rinehart.

This lady needed June's help in picking the yellow flower of a certain weed that grew near the baseball field. Mrs. Rinehart made her own pain-killer medicine. She dried the blossoms, crushed and mixed them with mineral oil and used the compound to ease the arthritic pains of her joints.

Deep wrinkles scored Mr. Sam Chapman's round face. This man whiled away the hours in pursuit of his hobby — he sculptured small objects with a pen knife. He carved peach seeds into monkey forms or shaped used toothbrush handles into small daggers. Starting with a two-foot long stick, he once carved a wooden chain that was over three feet long.

Mr. Williamson was a 66 year old man of average height. Dressed in his blue bib overalls, he looked the part of a farmer. This man came to live with us, but not at the request of an Odd Fellow lodge. When the Army bought his farm to build Camp Campbell, he had outlived all his kin-folks and had no place to go. The Army took not only the land that Mr. Williamson owned, but also that of many other area farmers. This added to the region's serious housing problem.

During the early stages of Camp Campbell, many of those who arrived daily could find no place to rent. They soon filled every empty house. Some workers slept in their cars. Mr. Williamson combed the area without finding a place before coming to us.

Mr. Widgery had taken over from Mr. Acree. The new superintendent moved all the old men and women to the main building to make room for new renters. Mr. Widgery had lived in Memphis and Mr. Williamson had spent several decades farming. The latter made an offer that would serve both parties. For a small wage, plus room and board, he would come to work on the farm.

Above and beyond this job as straw-boss, Mr. Williamson played another role. The man was a stand-in grandfather to me. He lent me a sympathetic ear as I struggled through some tough times. My problems stemmed from changes linked to the passage into puberty. I tended to anger and to blow up too easily. I welcomed the chance to discuss this with an adult, one who listened without a critical or negative response. He helped me muddle through those vexing days.

Doing the farm work with Mr. Williamson was fun. He related many anecdotes from his background, and delighted us with the special skills he had learned as a longtime farmer. The one action that charmed me above all others was the way he went into action upon seeing a snake.

One day, as we loaded a wagon with loose hay, a brown snake slithered from the field toward a nearby fence. Mr. Williamson simply reached down and grabbed the critter's tail, even though it was a poisonous copperhead. He swung his arm in a long circular sweep that built up a centrifugal force. This kept the snake from moving into a biting posture. Mr. Williams snapped as if to crack a whip, and the reptile's head popped off and soared through the air.

He often amused us with tales dating back to early days of the nineteen hundreds. One story dealt with the Night Riders, a group of tobacco growers who started an association. Their aim was to bring a higher price for their crops. Over the years, the alliance slowly changed and added to its mission. Mr. Williamson told how the secret group began to take an interest in the morals of the area's families.

He told how they worked. If a man drank and beat his wife, the Night Riders forced him to show respect for his family. If a man gambled to excess, or engaged in other bad conduct that caused him to neglect his wife and children, they paid him a visit. A hooded rider gave the man a verbal warning about what might happen if he refused to alter his ways. The riders visited a second time if the night visitor's first trip failed to cause a change.

According to Mr. Williamson, a midnight flogging would persuade the man to change his ways. They wore masked hoods, but the Night Riders didn't identify with the Ku Klux Klan. At times I wondered if Mr. Williamson rode with the Night Riders to help keep others straight. Did he gain the knowledge as the target of a late night visit? That remains a mystery — he didn't admit to having been a Night Rider.

Until he left the orphanage, less than two years after he came, the farm straw-boss thrilled us with his exciting tales. The other old folks told their stories too.

Although the orphanage housed both children and aged people, it was not a nursing home. Most of our older men and women enjoyed good health. They spent hours talking with one another. From their porch swings and chairs, they watched the younger children at play on the seesaws, in the sand box or on the small merry-go-round.

Unlike the children, the aged people could come and go as they pleased. They enjoyed a good life without the rigors of earning their keep. The basic needs of food, shelter and clothing were met, but was not enough. Like all humans without regard to age, they hungered for, and needed, a measure of self-esteem and approval. The boss, and children alike, met this vital need by showing the old folks a proper respect.

The aged residents talked about their former pursuits. I listened to these stories and used the details to help set my own goals. How would I manage my life, plan for my advanced years? I wanted to avoid the need of having to rely on the good will of others. I hoped to shun charity at the end of my working days.

Because of these nostalgic tales by the elderly I often returned to those thoughts that had come to me in the corn field as a thirteen-year old boy. On that hot summer afternoon, I decided not to become a farmer. I resolved to learn how to use my mind to earn a living, without having to depend on physical labor. It would be: Brain Power instead of Brawn Power.

The years slowly eased by as my resolve strengthened. I would try to avoid the fate that many of the old folks faced. I saw them as being trapped, isolated from family and dependent on others. A common theme seemed to grip a few of them — devoid of hope, they brooded about their final days. This gloomy spirit clashed with my forward-looking hopes.

The passage of time should bring a better life! That's how I looked at my own situation. I could not deal with this mind-set the old folks held. To me it was pathetic. However, I listened keenly to the endless stories they told and saw that they loved to talk with young people.

I was too immature then to accept the thought of death. A teenager cannot, or at least will not, concern himself about his own mortality. I didn't. A youngster in the spring of life thinks differently than one in the winter of his being.

Even though our outlooks differed, my delight in the old folks' tales increased as I moved into the teen years. My respect for our half-dozen remaining older men and women increased. I began to see the true nature of my own thought process. My ideas of youth and vigor had led me to a warped idea. I spent little time thinking about death, but knew that people died when they reached old age.

When one of the old folks passed away, we opened a grave in the Home's cemetery and held a funeral. A quartet of girls sang *Rock of Ages* or *In the Garden* at the service. My teenage thoughts centered on life, not death. I refused to see myself in that situation.

I found many chances to observe and discuss this with the old folks when I brought the coal that fueled their fireplaces. This job gave me daily contacts with them, during the last couple of years. We had shut down the central power plant, so the coal-burning hearths furnished the heat in their living quarters. The old folks lived on the main building's first and second floors.

Depending on the weather, I lugged eight to ten buckets of coal daily to the grates. In the role of a male Cinderella, I scooped the ashes from the fireplaces. This chore, which I did before and after school, was painful, but it had some pleasing side effects besides my talks with the old folks.

The heavy work helped to expand my arm, leg and shoulder muscles, a big plus in my training for high school football. Many books given to the orphanage, sat in the rows of bookcases that lined the upper floor hall. My favorite was the *Book of Knowledge*. A small light, barely enough to read by, filtered from the sun porch into the hallway. I thumbed through the books until I found something to hold my interest.

A broad smile on the old folks' face usually welcomed the supply of fuel I brought. These contacts helped me to decide several goals for my life as I often asked them for advice during the visits. When I put certain questions to some of these folks, their eyes would brighten. They would come up with a number of good ideas. Others were different.

Mrs. Jesse Adair and Mrs. Laura Mannen occupied rooms next to each other. Both were about the same age and were widows of Odd Fellows, but the similarity ended there. Mrs. Adair had a nimble mind, and was ready to discuss any subject. Her opinions spread over a wide range of subjects, from the weather — to the war and the way the country was moving.

On the other hand, the passive and moody Mrs. Mannen talked very little. She often failed to acknowledge me until I greeted her. Slouching in the chair and silently gazing at the fireplace, Mrs. Mannen, it seemed to me, wanted to protect her thoughts. My daily visits seemed to disturb this veil of melancholy, to pull her away from the solitude she wished. Her lethargy, the dimly lit room and the gray winter day all acted in concert to lay down the scene of despair and gloom.

"Oh, thanks for bringing the coal, Buddy," she would say, after she collected her thoughts.

I tried several times, but she always turned down my attempts at conversation. I wondered if the lady had given up on life. She apparently had — about a month after I left the orphanage, she passed away.

Mrs. Adair showed a lively spirit, one that allowed her sunny nature to shine even on a cloudy day. She would ask, as I removed the ashes from her fireplace,

"How did school go today — Tell me what you learned in each class?"

I liked this show of interest. Maybe the time we spent did little more than dispel her loneliness, but these exchanges lifted my spirits. I gained a higher level of insight and vision from her views on the diverse topics. She offered some important guidance that helped me focus my thoughts and set future goals.

Mrs. Adair's room became my favored spot for resting and warming myself between trips to and from the coal bin. This unique person was a well schooled, prim and proper dowager. She had read a broad body of subjects. We talked about many of them in our chats; she always told me that I'd need to learn many things. This, I had already known before I began to deliver the coal.

Mrs. Adair and I often discussed the obstacles that stood in the way of my going to college. Wishing only to toughen my resolve, she mentioned the snags I would face.

"You'll need money to buy books and pay fees. You'll need to study long hours, but most importantly, you'll need to make a long term commitment."

"Making it through college will be a long and hard task," she said from her erect sitting posture.

"It will only happen if you want it with all your heart."

"I do want it," I told her, and also told myself again and again.

With high school graduation at hand, and my looking forward to a new life outside the orphanage, I thanked Mrs. Adair for the advise and encouragement she had given me. She and the other old folks helped me a great deal. I like to think that we helped each other.

Chapter 8

Music

His receding hairline and mustache belied his age. Band director Gilbert (Pete) William's was 26 years old. He arrived in 1933, one year after our family had entered the orphanage. Pete was Mrs. Acree's cousin. This family tie brought him to the orphanage where he drew a salary of fifteen dollars per month plus room and board. This was good pay during the Great Depression when work of any type was difficult to find.

Highly qualified, Pete was not only a great musician but also a good organizer. His father, who for several years had directed a brass band in Bumpus Mills, Tennessee, taught Pete to play the trumpet. Like his father, Pete seemed destined to become a band leader. His job required that he start a band and teach music to the children.

Pete helped to continue a tradition, for the orphanage had sponsored bands and choral groups over the years. Under his guidance a new band, with a membership that ranged from twenty to thirty boys and girls, became a spirited organization. His nine-year tenure as band director ended in 1942, during which time the Orphanage's population of boys and girls steadily dwindled. With only forty or so remaining by the early forties, Pete chose the prospects from fewer and fewer children.

Most towns in Middle Tennessee supported a musical group during the early part of the century, and many had a marching band. People wanted live music, so they built band stands for concerts. The community bands filled a void.

These bands of unpaid music makers often formed the nucleus of civic life in small towns. They showed up in the town parades as marching bands or drum and bugle corps. They served as the focal point for the Fourth of July sports as well as Decoration (Memorial) Day and Armistice (Veterans) Day events.

The music-making group was as much a community fixture as its baseball team. At the orphanage, both our marching band and ball teams gave a sense of great pride.

My older sister, June, played the French horn. We dubbed the instrument a "peck horn," since that describes the work it does. June stayed with the horn when she later enrolled in the Clarksville High School band. Pete had recruited her nearly a year before he tapped me to join the band.

When Barbara was six years old she became a miniature majorette. She and Mr. Acree's youngest daughter, Sara Grey, pranced and strutted ahead of the band's teen-age majorette. Brightly dressed, these tiny girls captured and held the spotlight as they twirled their small batons. From my vantage point in the columns, I judged from the spectators' smiles that these two were the stars of the marching band. When she was eight years old, Barbara changed to the cymbals, but later would play the clarinet. She stayed with it in the high school band.

Fred did not become a band member, for it would have interfered with his duties at the orphanage. His job at the dairy barn took precedence over music; someone had to stay home and milk the cows twice daily.

Pete invited me to join the band in 1937. He had asked most of the children, but a few turned him down. One boy flatly insisted that he did not want to learn to play the trumpet. Mr. Acree happening to hear this rebuff, intervened — this led to a serious conflict.

"You will learn to play the trumpet," said the boss to the reluctant one.

This approach didn't work, but Mr. Acree didn't let it drop. When the first effort failed to convince the boy, Mr. Acree issued an ultimatum.

"You will, and I'm giving you a week to think about it. Starting after school tomorrow, I want to get a trumpet and march on the road between the boys' building and the old folks' building. You are to march back and forth one hour a day until you decide to learn to play the horn."

Each day, the boy marched alone — up and down the road — tucked under his arm was the horn he wanted no part of. The reluctant trumpet player walked and thought about the impasse, all the while matching wits with the boss. The week passed and Mr. Acree's tactic had failed, for the boy still refused join the band. Pete disagreed with this method of gaining a band member, but said nothing.

I, myself, had no misgivings about joining the band. One day, before band practice, Pete said, "Buddy, I need another person in the rhythm section. How would you like to try out?"

"Sure," I said.

I agreed, knowing that from time to time the band practiced after school. This would free me from some of the farm work, so Pete's invitation struck me as a great idea. I could avoid some toil and learn to play an instrument besides.

At the first practice session Pete handed me a triangle, a device made from an iron rod bent to form three equal sides. I was to hold it by its leather handle and strike it with a steel-bar hammer.

Pete said, "Strike the triangle in rhythm with the music each time I point at you."

Except for its tiring my arm, the instrument was easy to play. I had only to watch Pete as he led the band. When the music called for a metallic tone, he pointed at me, and I rang the instrument to the beat of the music. During a break between numbers, the drummer who stood next to me showed me how to find the notes on the sheet music. After a few sessions, I could follow the score and tap without Pete's prompt.

Some two weeks later, Pete said to me

"I've been watching to see if you could keep the rhythm, and it looks like you can."

"I need someone on the bass horn. That's what I had in mind from the start. Would you like to play the tuba?"

"But, I can't read music."

"That's no problem — anyone can learn to read music," Pete assured me.

"Look, see the lines on this sheet of music? Some notes sit directly on the five lines. Each one has a name. Reading from the bottom up, they are G-B-D-F-A. Think: GOOD BOYS DO FINE ALWAYS, well, that's the name of the notes.

"The notes between lines have names too; they're F-A-C-E. When you play the bass horn, you use just a few of these."

It sounded simple enough. First, Pete showed me which hand valve to press to make each note. He then taught me how to blow the scales and told me to practice. This I did over and over. I had a bit of trouble hitting the correct notes on the big horn, but Pete soon let me to join the others. I felt proud to be a part of the band, and was happy with my progress, although I still hit a sour note now and then.

All went okay until the day Pete scheduled the first outside marching session. With the frame of a normal nine-year old boy, I had trouble supporting the big horn, marching and blowing all at the same time. Pete saw my struggle.

"Buddy, bring the base horn here and put it down on the grass."

He ended my tuba assignment on the spot. I stood there, dejected and watched the band march along the road away from the boys' building. They turned around at the old folks building and returned, stepping to the beat of *The Stars and Stripes Forever*.

Pete found a place for me to the percussion section, first at the cymbals. He later moved me to the snare drum and found my niche — I stayed with the drum.

The band held its practice sessions in the school auditorium. We rehearsed after school and before supper, but most often during the evenings. For me, the band offered a welcome change from chores and the usual farm work. I still had kitchen chores. No question about it, I enjoyed band practice.

Although we played mostly marches, Pete would sometimes select one or two popular tunes for a concert. Now and then, while working through a practice session or even on stage, we tried a piece from the classics. Pete took up the new musical types because he wanted us to expand our skills.

Whether in concert or when marching, we wore tall plumed hats, red silk shirts and red pants with a white stripe. The bright uniforms, the high-stepping majorettes and the stirring march all blended to create a flashy presence. We marched in columns of 3 or 4 abreast and it was always a problem to keep the lines straight.

The Fourth of July, Armistice Day and Christmas parade gave us the opportunity to march in local events. Those who rode on the floats ahead of the band often pitched candy to the people who lined the streets. I could not leave the march to chase the goodies, oh how I wanted to go after the candy. This, along with my never getting to see the parades, were my only regrets for being in the band.

A few Odd Fellow lodges asked the band to come and perform. One day we gave a concert at Chattanooga. After we played, Mr. Acree stepped on the stage and introduced us, saying a few words about each person. When he came to me, he pointed and said,

"Buddy keeps the fire going in the cook stove and washes the pots and pans."

I worked as the kitchen boy at the time, a job in which I did a number of tasks.

He moved to my sister Barbara and said,

"And here's Barbara, our little biscuit maker."

After he finished the introductions, the people clapped. They began to empty their pockets and pitch coins onto the low stage. Maybe it was our good manners, but no one moved to retrieve the coins. For me it was the bad feelings that came with being an object on display. I refused, even after Mr. Acree told us to pick up the coins at our feet. The people sensed the insult and seemed to be sorry.

The Author at Norris, Tennessee

Our band played at the Tennessee Valley Authority's Norris Dam grand opening near Knoxville. Although Fred was not in the band, he came along on this 1937 trip. Mr. Acree allowed June, Barbara, Fred and me to spend a few days with our mother and grandparents. This was the one and only visit during my fifteen years at the orphanage.

Each year the people of Pulaski, a town in the middle of the state, asked that we join their parade on Memorial Day. We then called this pageant Decoration Day. It was a time to show respect for the fallen heroes. The parade formed near the burial grounds and marched to downtown.

This was my first visit to Pulaski and the first parade since my moving to the snare drum.

Pete gave me a little pep talk, saying,

"Buddy, this is a very special march. We are here to honor our dead heroes, so I want you to set a proper tone with your drum. We need a slow, solemn beat with perfect rhythm. When the band marches to your beat, the people all along the route will think of their loved ones."

I sensed that Pete's advice was sincere and I felt an obligation to set the day's mood and spirit. I wanted my drumsticks to give voice to a feeling that the crowd on the Pulaski streets could sense. Using every ounce of skill at my command, I struck a solemn rhythm. It seemed to work — the people along the street removed their hats and stood in silence as we marched by.

Our band paid a visit to Columbia, Tennessee each year, where they held an affair known as Mule Day. A giant mule market, a super parade and a grand display of goods for sale marked this April event. With those from other towns, our band joined the thousands of people drawn to the town for the function.

Other than these two annual events, we played at many local functions. In the spring of 1941, we gave a concert for the grade-school graduation. All the 8th grade classes in the city and county met at Roosevelt School on Highway 41W South. My sister June not only played with our band that night. She stood out, in her bright red band attire, when she graduated with her class.

One day we struck up a snappy tune at the local court house and a big group of people drew near the band. We played for one reason — publicity, to attract a crowd. After two or three numbers, Percy Priest, a young man running for U. S. Congress for the first time, spoke to the crowd from the courthouse steps. He won the race, went to Washington and stayed there for many terms.

We made day trips, and at times journeys of more distance, where we stayed overnight. I enjoyed these longer travels the most.

A group of Rebekahs, the ladies' arm of the Odd Fellows, asked to have our band play at their state meeting in Birmingham. This trip to Alabama held great prospects for the band members, and in a way it topped our dreams. There were many things to see, including the giant statue of Vulcan that stood on Red Mountain above the city.

That evening some fifteen Rebekah drill teams contended for the winner's ribbon. Each group marched to our band music. They made turns in perfect unison, criss-crossed the room single file and came back together as a unit. The judges graded each drill team that took the spotlight and stepped lively across the floor. Each group seemed to prefer the same tune, Offenbach's *Barcarole,* and my patience began to wear thin. The evening grew longer, and I thought, "Surely this next group will end the contest," but then a new team stepped out of the wings.

The contest ran well past the midnight hour, and we played the same tune more than ten times. It's a perfectly good piece of music, thanks, but I'll choose something else. The melody has worn out. I would just as soon forget the music-making part of the Birmingham trip.

The trip to Alabama, like the others, gave me some new points of view. A journey to come a bit later, however, would top all the others. In April of 1941, Mr. Acree announced that, in June, the band would go on a two-week tour of Florida.

Repairs to the bus delayed the trip until July. We drove to Montgomery, Alabama the first day. That afternoon, I stood where Jefferson Davis took the oath of office as the Confederate President. A bronze star, embedded in the concrete step at the state capitol, marks the site. After our first concert that evening, we split into groups of two or three and spent the night in the homes of local Odd Fellows.

We gave the first Florida concert in Tallahassee and headed south the next morning. It surprised me that such a small town could be the state's capital. The Odd Fellow lodges along our route, not only sponsored our concerts but also supplied a fired-up crowd to hear us.

By day we visited the tourist sights and played concerts in the evenings. When we came to the Suwannee River, Mr. Acree stopped the bus and allowed us to take a closer look at the water-way made famous by song. Surprisingly, the water was the color of tar. I later learned that the plants that line the banks still cause this condition.

The Band at St. Petersburg, Florida; Mr. Acree and Pete Williams at left on back row; Barbara third from left on front row; June first and Author third from right on 2nd row.

We had many thrills in Florida. A streamliner train, its whistle blaring, zipped past our bus as we drove along a west coast high-way. The passengers returned my waves as I watched the train in awe. The coal-fired engines of the Tennessee trains belched plumes awe. The coal-fired engines of the Tennessee trains belched plumes of black smoke. This train's roaring diesel engine pulled it without the smoke.

I had never seen a bridge as long as the one that spanned the bay between St. Petersburg and Tampa. I saw a docked seagoing ship as we rode past the harbor — another first. We traveled through the mid-state citrus zone where bright oranges adorned the groves of lush green trees that covered the hills. We heard the organ music at Bok Tower, the famous traveler's rest near Lake Wales.

Working 13 of the 14 nights on tour, the band played before about one hundred people per concert. Our largest audience came to hear us at a St. Petersburg park. We also drew a large Daytona Beach crowd to our concert at the ocean bandstand.

The travel plans called for our arrival at the concert venue in the afternoon. This allowed time to split into groups and meet with our hosts so they might receive us into their homes that night. The local folks were to meet us at the school grounds the evening we were to play at Leesburg. We arrived a bit early and found the school grounds deserted.

As we unloaded our instruments I saw several ripe oranges hanging from the limbs of a tree. I wondered why this fruit still hung on a tree. Why hadn't the students already picked the oranges? I decided to pick myself an orange or two after the concert. The night's darkness would cover me.

So, that evening, I climbed the tree eager to pick my first orange. Large thorns grew on the branches, but I persisted and eagerly plucked two pieces of fruit. Back on the ground, I peeled an orange and popped a section into my mouth. What a jolt to my taste buds; the fruit was too sour to eat. I learned later that this citrus tree thrives due to its hardy root system. Though its oranges are worthless, other strains of better-tasting fruit do well when grafted to the tree. It's no wonder the students allowed the oranges to stay on the tree.

The next day, Mr. Acree bought a bushel of oranges at a roadside stand. He placed them at the front of the bus and said,

"Eat as many as you wish."

I ate a half dozen before stopping for I had never eaten oranges that tasted so good. They were fresh and juicy, not shriveled and dried like the lone orange we found in our Christmas stockings during the 30's and 40's.

We saw the ocean at Daytona Beach for the first time. The beautiful blue waters of the Atlantic seemed to draw us. When we approached to swim, the sun-baked sand gave me the hotfoot. However, my biggest shock at the beach came when I first romped and plunged into the surf. I had not counted on the salty water stinging my eyes and mouth. The July sun burnt my tender skin in short order. The pain and blisters lasted two days. Beyond that, the dry and peeling skin continued to pester me a week later.

My biggest surprise of the Florida tour came from another source. It involved our staying in the homes of Odd Fellow lodge members. At each town the band would split into groups of two or three people and spend the night as guests of these folks. This was the case except the one night that we stayed at Orlando's Angebilt Hotel. Our hosts opened their homes and supplied three meals, including lunch for the next day.

The visits allowed me to see how the members of a household lived under ideal settings. At age thirteen, all this impressed me. I savored the feeling of life in a normal home. The most pleasant part was their relaxed way of dining — I compared it to the harsh regimented system of the orphanage. They all handled themselves in a casual manner ease during the meals. The children eagerly joined the discourse and seemed to have an equal footing with the adults.

The hosts offered us china plates and real glasses instead of aluminum plates and tumblers. The types of food served, as well as the beds they supplied, impressed me. They divided the clean-up chores and reacted with each other in a cheerful manner. All this stood in stark contrast to my life. Although I enjoyed the time with our hosts, it added to the conflict growing inside me. I longed to live a normal family life in a loving home.

In short, the customs that I observed in the twelve private homes began to prey on my mind. The visits stirred some fond thoughts from long ago — when at age four, I lived a joy-filled life with my mother and father. As I recalled those good times, I loathed my present life even more.

This fresh view of our host's lifestyles caused me to think of the future. It provoked an appetite for more freedom. I longed for the time when Mr. Acree would no longer run my life and yearned to strike out on my own. As a direct result of the Florida trip, this craving grew in me until it had colored my entire outlook.

The band trip ended with an evening concert in Jacksonville, and we headed home the next morning. With Pete and Mr. Acree taking turns at the wheel of the bus, we traveled all day and arrived late that night.

About six months after the Florida band tour, Pete joined millions of other Americans and answered a draft call. Given the dwindling numbers at the orphanage, the band could not have lasted beyond the early part of 1942.

Pete could make beautiful music with his trumpet. Its sweet melody and perfect rhythm called for all within earshot to pick up the beat. None but the unfeeling could resist. The guests at our concerts approved with their applause, often stopping the show when Pete played a solo. He could play many styles of music — jazz, blues or a lively version of *The Washington Post March*. After the war end, Pete joined the Jimmy Mansfield Orchestra, a well-known band of the mid forties. After touring a few years, it served as house band at the same radio station that gave Lawrence Welk his start. Later, Pete would finish college and become master of the Fort Campbell High School Band.

Pete's eight years of work at the orphanage endured. He gave me, along with many other young boys and girls, a love of music. It would last a lifetime.

Other Music

Three trends seem to have helped replace the demand for community bands and other forms of live music. In the forties, people turned to their radios for music. The growth of popular musical movies marked this trend too. Adding to these changes, after the war, records burst on the scene.

At the orphanage we were able to pick up the Nashville radio stations. Most of the time, their broadcasts consisted of country music. Unless one played an instrument, heard records or saw a movie, this was the local area's chief source of music.

The New York Metropolitan Opera came on Saturday afternoons. I liked the program, although I could not follow the opera's story line. The other boys ribbed me about my love of the 'long hair stuff.' Perhaps it was the teasing that inspired and touched the stubborn streak in me. Perhaps it was the emotion in the music. In any event, I looked forward to the operas with vocals so full of passion.

The area had no broadcast station until after the war. Besides the country music, Radio Station WJZM brought jazz, pop and the big band sound to the area.

The AM radio signals of the times suffered from a major fault. With even a slight weather problem the sounds cracked through the charged air and laced the music with static. The reception seemed to improve late at night. Then we picked up signals from as far away as New Orleans or Cincinnati. Popular music and the big band sounds prevailed on these stations.

We had one other music source — a large hand cranked record player. Someone had donated the machine and a few 78 RPM discs. The machine must have arrived when Mr. Acree was there, but not until Mr. Byrom came were we allowed to use it. The difference between these two men came in sharp focus as we made good use of the device.

It sat in the dining room where it gave hours of untold pleasure. The hard-rubber records were about a quarter-inch thick; and if dropped, they either cracked or shattered into many pieces. We played the records even though they might have a crack or scratch. Many opera tunes were among the stack of discs that offered a world of music other than country.

Soon after he came, Mr. Byrom allowed the girls to sponsor a dance in the dining room. It gave us hope that he would okay such an event. I had just entered high school. The strict regiment had ended. We now began to live a new lifestyle, more like other people. We celebrated this by singing. Our songs picked up and expressed this newfound joy.

At dusk we sat in the front porch swing and sang, as if to entertain the fireflies that sparkled above the rich green lawn. Boys and girls, lifting their voices in song, harmonized a cheerful welcome to the changes. In this joyous mood, we sang old favorites such as *I've Been Working on the Railroad,* or *Jimmy Crack Corn.* We belted out with *The Old Gray Mare Ain't What She Used to Be* or vocalized a well-known tune of the day, such as *The White Cliffs of Dover.*

> This lively spirit gave our songs a sparkle of freedom that music alone can express.

We often sang these and others songs at sunset. The music mirrored the hope and joy in our hearts. Our music proclaimed the new climate that the Byroms brought to the orphanage. This lively spirit gave our songs a sparkle of freedom that music alone can express.

Chapter 9

Holidays and Religion

Christmas

Like any young child, I looked forward to each pending big event with hopeful suspense. Examples of these for me were a band trip, the day the boss allowed us to shed our shoes for the summer and Christmas time. This focus on future delights was much more than a simple longing. It helped to think of something better in the future, for that was better than dealing with the present.

Christmas was tops. Every child at the orphanage looked forward to the season's joy and delight. The stir began a month before the big day. That's when Mr. Acree asked each child what he or she wanted for Christmas.

We could name three things. My tense joy increased as the boss wrote down a scooter, a cowboy suite or a red wagon as the main gift. We knew not to place great hope in our receiving the big item of the request, for there was a limit to the gift. An older boy, when nearly ready to leave the orphanage, might ask for a dress suit. The boss viewed that gift as the entire three-item request, jacket, vest and pair of trousers.

Given the limit to the size of our gift, luck was with us if Santa brought the shiny Radio Flyer wagon or new scooter. Along with the main and two smaller presents, we received a standard favor year after year. Stuffed in each boy or girl's red-mesh stocking, was a bit of hard candy, a box of raisins plus an apple or orange.

I savored the orange in a special way. First, I squeezed and rolled the fruit between my hands until it softened, and then cut a hole in the top. After removing the crook from a red and white candy cane, I plunged in the straight part. The candy stick became a make-shift straw. I'd suck all the juice from the fruit, caressing my taste buds with the flavor of peppermint-orange.

Until 1941, with the orphanage in its heyday, we packed into the school's auditorium for the Christmas program. Though we put out extra chairs, our visitors often had to stand in the back of the room. Gifts from the Odd Fellows and Rebekahs, their lady's groups, from across the state helped to make the event a success. A Rebekah group might give a bushel of apples or oranges. Another would offer a box of candy. These folks often brought the items to help us keep the holiday.

We held this affair on the Sunday before Christmas, allowing people to visit with us and still have their Christmas Day at home. Our program featured a group of the smaller boys and girls in a Christmas skit. The children sang carols. The main event came when Santa entered and handed out the gifts.

The guests arrived from throughout the state. Our mother came to a couple of these galas. She came when I, at age six, had the first part in a Christmas program. I performed before the group of nearly two hundred people. Though frightened by the prospect of facing a crowd, I learned the verse, stood on the stage and spoke my lines as I rubbed my stomach. The words of the ditty still rest on the tip of my tongue:

> Christmas cookies, yum, yum, yum,
> Don't you wish that you had some?

Soon after the skit portion of the routine ended, Santa Claus would make his big entrance. An air of happy excitement filled the room as the time neared, but first Mr. Acree would introduce a high profile person. The guest always made a long speech. The talk, coming in the program when it did, was like a TV station cutting in to tout a new toothpaste while your team runs a touchdown. We were eager for Santa to arrive.

A thunderous roar hailed Santa when he bounded into sight of the children. He carried on his back a big sack filled with un-wrapped toys. Each present bore a tag with a child's name. Santa called out the name and handed the item to his helper for distribution. Each gift brought a broad smile to the child's face. I could hardly wait for that special name to be called — mine.

This was the best moment of the Christmas Holiday. From about the age of nine, however, I began to have some strange feelings. This had little to do with the season, but more with what I read into the nature of the guests. With these feelings running deep,

I began to think of the program as a side show. I thought the boss had displayed us in exchange for the guest's charity.

In the forties, when forced by their state of affairs to accept help, most people felt a certain shame. Hard as it was to admit being poor, it was much more stressful when a person had to receive a gift in a public setting. As I moved into my teens, I felt the sting of this shame each time the crowd watched me take a gift.

Fewer guests came because of the wartime fuel needs. When the renters moved into the former boys' building, we held the Christmas program in the dining hall. We still sang carols around the Christmas tree, but the events lacked their former luster and detail. With fewer children, the programs waned.

Each year in mid December we still went to the woods at Garretts and cut a tall cedar tree. We adorned it with lights, ornaments and strings of popcorn. In 1942, the year I turned fourteen, the act of bringing in the Christmas tree was an event to remember.

We had selected the tree, loaded it on a wagon pulled by a team of mules and brought it to the dining room's front door. The doors opened from the inside and mules suddenly bolted. We tried to regain control of the runaway team, but the harness reins danced out of reach. The other boy and I were in for a wild ride, so we held tightly to the wagon. The team headed straight for a large tree. One mule went to the right, the other went to the left and the wagon tongue struck the tree dead center. Our ride ended with a loud thud.

The impact threw the tree and both boys to the ground. Thankfully, the wild ride injured neither the mules, the Christmas tree nor the riders.

Easter

A great deal of effort marked the orphanage's yearly Easter egg hunt. On Saturday the girls boiled and colored a supply of eggs for the hunt.

The older girls and boys, each playing the role of Easter Bunny during the noon meal, went to the front lawn and hid the hard-boiled and candy eggs. They buried the prizes in clumps of grass or placed them behind trees.

On Easter Sunday, after the bell rang to end the midday meal, the boys and girls dashed from the dining hall to the front lawn. The fastest runners and older children found the most eggs. After the hunt, the superintendent required the ones who found the bulk of goodies to share their haul with the others.

When I was small I couldn't run fast enough to find many prizes, so I liked the sharing idea. Later, after growing older and being able to find more than my portion of the eggs, I resented being forced to give them away. Had not I found the treasures myself? Why should I share?

One day, when I was a teen, Mr. Byrom asked me to play the Easter Bunny. As I hid the eggs I realized that it was only fair to divide the Easter eggs with the small children so they could share in the fun.

Worship

By instinct and regard for detail, I learned a few things on my own, but needed some help with matters of the spirit. The Odd Fellows Home did not claim ties with any church, but the superintendents served up a steady diet of worship.

We prayed before each meal. On Sunday morning we attended Sunday School in our dining room. Mr. Acree taught the older children, while his wife held class for the younger boys and girls. A company that printed the texts for a number of Protestant churches supplied the lesson guides that we used. Mr. Acree made every child attend Sunday School, but I didn't resent this.

I looked forward to the Bible stories. In addition, I delighted in the way Miss Frances read to us in our regular school class. She read from the Bible every day. Despite my love of these stories, from the age of eleven onward, I began to loathe being forced by Mr. Acree to attend church service. That was a different matter.

Each Sunday evening, from the time I was seven, he loaded us in the bus and drove to Clarksville to attend church. If they held service on Sunday evenings, we would drop in on them — Baptist,

Christian, Church of Christ, Methodist or Zionist, it didn't matter. We rotated — a new church was our target each week.

> My dread of these church visits had nothing to do with our exposure to religion. I cringed at our carnival-like entrances.

My dread of these church visits had nothing to do with our exposure to religion. I cringed at our carnival-like entrances. I hated it when a preacher gave a welcome speech as we marched down the aisle to the front-row seats. I wondered if Mr. Acree had planned to arrive after the service had started that we could make a high-profile entrance. Often, a minister would stop his sermon and make a spectacle of us, saying,

"Brother Acree, we want to welcome you, and all your little orphans, to our service tonight."

One preacher would say,

"We're so proud to welcome Brother Acree and all his little Or-finks."

I was not an orphan; I had a mother. Perhaps this fact caused me to view the patronizing welcome with total contempt. We sub-teens soon picked up on the wording. We referred to each other, when safely out of earshot of the boss, as Brother Acree's little "Or-finks."

These talk-down remarks by the preacher made a sham of our visit. I felt like a freak in a sideshow, with every eye in the building aimed straight at the back of my head. After taking a seat in the church, I wanted to duck under the pew. I'd do anything to avoid the curious stares of the other people in the church.

An emotional storm raged inside me as I lived through these events. I deeply resented this aspect of the worship service. Though difficult to put in words, I can easily get in touch with those feelings that troubled me.

Perhaps Mr. Acree put our group on display to gain the good will of the church members. This thought triggered some strong negative feelings deep within me. As an anxious pre-teen boy, I yearned for nothing more than to look normal. I deeply resented the thought of my being an object on display. Living in the orphanage had made me super sensitive to this point.

In spite of my hating this aspect of our church visits, I gained more from attending than I realized. Easing into my mid-teen years, I started to pay attention to the sermons. I even took notes. I often tried to discern and list the main points of the preacher's message. This routine helped me to focus on matters of the spirit. Truth and logic often crossed the preacher's lips, and their ideas began to take hold.

New thoughts came to mind, even though I gained them in church while under duress. Many times I wished not to be in church. If not there, perhaps I would have missed the spiritual factor that has added much value to my life. About this time, and I was fifteen, my outlook toward living in the orphanage began to soften.

After Mr. Acree left, we could decide for ourselves whether to attend a church or not. I paid a visit to the New Providence Baptist Church and soon went there on a weekly basis. Only a mile away, it was within an easy walking distance. The church's active youth program lured several boys and girls from the orphanage.

I started to read the Bible daily, and went to church for both the Sunday morning and evening services. Beyond my needs of the spirit, the effort filled some of my desires of a social nature. I met and made new friends with people outside the orphanage. Soon, the minister asked me to take a role in the work of the church's young people. Leading the lessons and making the class reports to the church, I learned to speak before a crowd without stage fright. This tie-in with the Baptist Young People's Training Union helped to bring a new direction to my life.

At age fifteen, a landmark event helped to prompt this change and set me on the new course. One afternoon after school, as I walked to the Garretts pasture to bring in the milk cows, two chipmunks appeared on the path. They darted out of the brush some twenty feet ahead. I wanted to watch the critters, so I sat on a large limestone rock and waited for them to appear again.

The chipmunks failed to show themselves, but while resting there I slipped into a strange mystical mood. My daydreams roamed and soon focused on life itself — my life. The thrust of these musings took a turn toward the spiritual aspect of my life. These thoughts stirred some new ideas and questions. Two main questions seemed to stick in my mind:

Who am I?

Why am I here?

I tried to make sense of these questions, but failed. Wishing to hold on to a stable mental state, I struggled to find a way around the impasse. I searched back into my life history, but found nothing to help. I sat there on the stone trying to absorb, or at the least, to control these strange new thoughts. I soon became agitated by thinking about the questions. The answers never came, for there were none.

With these thoughts, I soon sensed the nature of the moment. I was in the middle of a religious event. The curious matters buzzed through my head. My audible request for help rang out, as I appealed to Jesus. Suddenly an invisible presence loomed around me. I tensed at the thought of His Spirit being so near, but my mind eased at once. The agitation that I endured faded, leaving me in a state of utmost peace. Filled with this new-found feeling of warmth and security I left Garretts that day a changed person.

With the incident fresh in mind, I became a member of the church. This closer personal walk with the Divine brought me a perfect bliss and freedom. Never before had I known such peace. A sense of nurture began to replace the vague feeling that something was missing from my life. I entered a new sphere — one purged of all those feelings of trouble and distress. My entire outlook began to improve.

Chapter 10
Fun Times

Life at the orphanage had its redeeming moments. Feelings of complete bliss filled some of the days; as youngsters we spent many hours at play. I welcomed these occasions and the joy they brought for they added a much needed balance to my many troubles. The fun times helped compensate for the darker side of life at the orphanage.

One day a grown man dressed in a cowboy suit stood on our front lawn. He towered over the crowd of boys and girls around him. The big white hat and familiar face attracted the children. Tom Mix came and invited us to his show in New Providence that very afternoon. Mr. Acree agreed.

This well-known movie star of the thirties toured the country with his circus. Tom Mix always invited the children at the local orphanages to attend his show free of charge. Astride his horse Tony Junior, he galloped into view of an audience made up of our people and other happy children from the area. We roared as he began to perform his riding and roping tricks.

Thanks to the movies, he was already a hero in our eyes. From time to time, the Clarksville theater owner let us view a movie free except for the state tax. On Saturdays, they ran serials that continued the following week. To hook the kids, the picture would end at the height of a thrilling moment. We wanted to come back the next time, for our hero faced a dreadful risk at the end of each segment.

Sometimes the anti-hero tied the lead actor to a railroad track as a train raced around the bend. Maybe the hero was in a gun battle. He had shot several bad guys, before running out of bullets. Now, a host of villains closed in for the kill. We described this type movie as a 'Shoot'em Down and Stack'em Up.' The star always prevailed, but how would he escape unharmed at the start of next week's show? We counted ourselves lucky if we caught the next chapter.

During the early forties, Carl Mann ran the projector at the Clarksville movie house. He dated and later married my sister June.

Carl allowed me to view many films through a small window in the projection room.

While growing up, we often designed and made our own crude toys for entertainment. A boy might build a pair of stilts by nailing a triangular scrap of wood to two long sticks. Soon, every boy stood three feet taller and walked around perched on the gadget he had made. A home-made plaything might hold our interest for a week or two before something else took its place.

We made slingshots, and were always looking for a well-shaped 'Y' in a tree limb. After cutting the limb to form a handle, we sliced rubber strips from an old inner tube and tied them to each fork of the stem. We used the flippers for target practice, holding contests to see who was the best shot or the first to knock a can off a fence post.

We staged many contests of skill with arrows and bows made from hickory saplings. Bull whips, made from leather, cracked to show off both loudness and expert aim. Good control took hours of rehearsal. A boy held a strip of paper in his hand, and his partner popped the strip in two. With an excellent aim, one could snap the whip without hitting the helper.

For many, mumblety-peg was a favorite pastime. This sport used a pocket knife with two opened blades. A player flipped the knife from his hand, foot or knee, and accrued points according to the way it stuck in the ground.

Hiking on Sunday afternoons was a great way to spend leisure time. We were both out of sight and on our own. A trek usually started when a couple of friends scrounged up some food and headed down to the L & N railroad tracks. The rails took us to a long wooden trestle that spanned a forty-foot deep ravine. Before crossing, we touched an ear to the steel rail and listened for vibrations. Hearing none, we could safely cross without getting caught on the bridge by a train.

Often on Sundays, we walked the mile to Garretts, a 100 acre parcel, where, as young boy, I enjoyed some of my greatest moments. The hills, dales and woodlands of this natural refuge helped us escape the watchful eye of the boss. A trip to this place was pure bliss. Once there, we played war games, made water wheels or gathered hickory nuts. From time to time, we organized a snake hunt or searched the twisting stream for crawfish, salamanders or minnows.

Of the three barns on the farm, the dairy barn offered the best chance for fun. We had a good reason to hang out there. A tin roof covered the hay loft, making it a good place to rest when rain kept us from working the fields. The effect of the rain was hypnotic. It beat down on the tin roof and serenaded us to sleep.

Rafters crisscrossed the upper story of the structure where we stored the hay. The cow's shed joined the back of the barn. This allowed us to feed the animals by simply pushing the hay through a rear door. With the hay below the rafters acting as a safety net, we learned to balance ourselves and walk ten feet above the floor. Moving along the four-inch wide girder was scary at first, but a bit of practice erased the panic. At times we amused ourselves in a game of tag, and zipped across the beams even with no hay below to break a fall.

In the later years, we baled the hay in the fields instead of storing it loose. These bales weighed about seventy pounds each and became good building blocks. We built rooms in the loft, connected them by tunnels and concealed the entrance way. This made an excellent place to hide.

The stock barn, located closer to the fields, offered other recreation. Its stables were home to our horses and mules. For several years, we tended sheep, sheared them each spring and sold the wool.

From time to time, when the boss wasn't around, we had fun with the sheep. We would drive two dozen bucks and ewes in the barn, closed the front and back breezeway doors and hold a riding contest. A boy would grab two handfuls of wool and ride as the sheep scattered. The winner was the one who could ride the big buck the longest time. This sport was great fun; luckily we didn't get caught.

Mr. Acree outlawed another sport, horse racing. In spite of this, one day Fred and I decided to have a race along the dirt lane that passed the stock barn. He was nine and I was twelve. The contest was to end at the orchard, some two hundred yards beyond the barn. Fred, riding Peanuts, a blue-tinted gray mare jumped off to a quick lead when a boy slapped his mount on the rump. With this surprise start, Fred dropped the bridle and lost control of the charging steed, but held on to the horse's mane. He pulled more than twenty feet ahead of me toward a sure win.

Although we were to race to the orchard, Peanuts had a different idea. Instead of running past the barn, she made a right sharp toward the barnyard. The gate was wide open. Fred tried to keep the speeding horse on course, but missed the entrance. They crashed into the opened gate. Peanuts stopped at once, but the momentum carried Fred forward. Across the gate he sailed, hitting the ground with a thud. When I reached him, he was out cold. In a few minutes he came around, but suffered from a nasty headache.

Fred spent the next few days quietly lying in a Clarksville hospital bed, nursing a concussion. The boss knew that he had fallen off Peanuts, but he didn't learn about the horse race.

We engaged in other acts of fun-seeking with better luck. No one suffered a serious mishap as we swam in the muddy waters of the Red River. The older boys had a strange way of teaching a nonswimmer to swim. They felt that throwing a beginner into the river was the best way for him to learn. Their motto was, "Sink, swim or float."

Having heard about this, I stayed away from the river, but many boys at the orphanage learned to swim by this high-risk and crude manner. Fortunately, I learned to swim in a more civilized manner. One hot summer day when I was eight, Mr. Acree took a group of boys and girls for a swim. He bused us to the spot where Peachers Mill Pike bridged the North Fork Creek.

The current swished rapidly along a twenty-foot section a few yards above the creek's well-used swimming hole. Standing at the foot of the rapids, Mr. Acree told us to step into the stream one at a time. As my turn came, I hesitated. Not until two girls had jumped in and floated down without a problem did I drum up enough courage to step forward. After a pausing and encouragement from the others, I plunged in and instantly zipped down the swift stream. Mr. Acree plucked me from the creek at the bottom.

"Go up there and try it again, Buddy, you just showed me that you can swim," said the boss.

I did, and it wasn't as scary the second time. Several more of the fun-filled splashes down the rapids convinced me that I had learned to swim. Soon I could go into the deeper parts of the pool without sinking.

Later, we often cooled ourselves in the Red River, less than a mile away. It mattered little to us if the rain and mud had tinted the water a reddish brown. Plunging in without a thought about water quality, we had come to have fun.

Our favorite place, now marked by a large limestone quarry, was a short distance upstream from where the Red flowed into the Cumberland River. Many tall trees lined both sides of the stream. As a magnet attracts iron, the river pulled us to the wonder world along its edges, a place any boy would love.

The Belly Buster

At the start of each summer we searched for a wild grape vine that hung over the water from a tree's branch. This made a great diving swing. If unable to find a natural vine to fit our purpose, we tied a rope to a tall limb. From a starting position high on the shore, one would grip the vine or rope, run downward to gain speed and swing out over the river. At the proper moment, we let go and plunge into the muddy water.

It was a warm day in late spring when I first tried this sport. At the urging of the other boys, I finally worked up enough courage to attempt the dive. I ran down the bank and sailed out across the muddy water only to plop into the river with a smashing belly buster. I had let go of the vine too soon. After a few more jumps, and learning to hold on until reaching the top of the arc, I could dive head-first into the water.

We made use of the river's muddy and steep banks, shaping the spot into a slide that allowed us to zip down the slope into the water. The Red River gave us many carefree moments, a great reward that came with growing up in the country.

We played tricks on each other. One day at dusk when I was nine years old, an older boy pointed to the squawking killdee birds that swooped by. He said to a group of younger boys, "Look at all those snipes. Does any one want to help me catch them. They're good to eat, you know."

It sounded like fun, so I asked, "How are we going to catch those birds?"

"It's easy," he answered. "They sleep in holes at night, so all we need do is to make the birds think they've found their hole for the night. Hold a gunny sack open, and they'll go straight for it. When one flies in, close the sack and you've got it."

He then explained the game plan: "It will be easier to fool the birds if the smaller boys hold the sacks."

I could hardly wait to take my position as the older boy led us to the edge of a black locust thicket. Speaking in a hushed and convincing voice he gave us more instructions.

"Be sure to hold the sack open wide when you see the birds."

Leaving three boys at the assigned spots near the wood's edge, he went to drive the snipes in our direction. We were to wait quietly and open the bags when the birds flew by.

I scanned the sky for killdees as the daylight faded into blackness. A few birds flew by now and then, but they failed to come near my opened sack. The milky way made its appearance. After an hour under the stars, I gave up on the birds and made my way back to the dorm. The last one to come in empty handed that night, I received a hardy ribbing from the crowd of boys.

"How many snipes did you catch?"

"How does it feel to be left holding the bag?" They gleefully quizzed.

This was only one of many times that the older boys had fun at my expense. I soon learned the rules that applied to having fun in a group. One prank stuck with me, or more to the point, I was the one stuck.

A railing made of six-inch diameter steel pipes edged the front steps and enclosed the porch of the boys' building. Ornamental iron globes sat on top of the posts where the railings met. One icy day, an older boy said,

"The best way to feel the cold of the frosty globe is to touch it with your tongue."

I pressed the metal sphere and promptly froze. I could not reclaim my tongue. The boys taunted me with a burst of laughter. Fortunately, my excited breath soon generated enough heat to free me. After this, I played this cold-day trick on the younger guys.

Like most teenage boys at the orphanage, at fourteen I wanted to drive the farm tractor. Before this, I had to persuade the one in charge to let me try. After dinner one day, this fellow drove another boy and me to the fields aboard the tractor. I hounded the driver with,

"Let me try my hand at the wheel."

After some intense nagging, he agreed.

"You'll have to wait until we get away from this fence, then I'll let you drive."

The dirt road leading to the work area hugged the fence, but we soon drove into the open field. At this spot, he stopped the tractor and I climbed into the big metal seat. I shifted gears and let out on the clutch and the machine jerked forward. At long last, I was driving, and it felt great to be behind the wheel.

We drifted to the left. Responding, I spun the big steering wheel to the right, but the machine refused to change course. That's because the front steel-rimmed wheels froze at a right angle. I had over corrected — the sudden jolt nearly threw the other passengers off the tractor. The engine almost stalled as we dug a six-inch deep furrow in our travel direction. The tutor, by stepping on the clutch, quickly ended my first attempt at driving.

After that, I closely watched the skilled driver. When he allowed me try the next time, I could hold the vehicle on course without over-steering. Months later, after many hours of practice on the tractor, I wanted to try driving our school bus.

Joe, a cotton-top boy about three years my senior, had just started high school. With the boss's okay, he drove the bus from the garage to the front road each school day. The other boys and girls boarded, and Mr. Acree drove them to school. He allowed Joe to learn by trial and error, but had forbid him to drive on the public roads.

He drove on the paved road anyway, but the boss didn't notice the dents Joe put on the bus when it scraped the neighbor's fence post. Fleming, another boy near the same age as Joe, also knew how to operate the bus, but I had never tried to drive it.

One evening after study hall, I saw Joe and Fleming talking in low tones. This sparked my curiosity, so moving closer to where they sat, I asked,

"What are y'all up to?"

"Nothing," Joe barked.

I could tell the question had irked him. "You don't have to bite my head off," I muttered. "I was only trying to make conversation."

"We're going to take a ride in the bus tonight, do you want to come along?" Fleming asked.

"Sure I do, where are we going?"

"No place special, maybe we'll drive out Peachers Mill Pike." Joe had calmed down, and I took this as an okay for me to tag along.

Later that night, an hour after lights out and the other boys in the dorm had gone to sleep, Joe slipped out of bed. Fleming and I followed his lead. I eased out of the nightgown and pulled on my clothes in the darkness. The three of us found our way down two flights of steps and stumbled through the pitch-dark basement. We exited the building's rear door on which there was no lock.

Donning our jackets, we stepped out into the frigid, but calm, night air. The stars of the Milky Way, sparkling against the moonless black sky, cast their weak light.

Fleming softly said to Joe,

"Do you have the key?"

"No, but it's in the bus."

We walked along the rear wall under the fire escape, crossed the driveway to the garage and climbed into the parked bus. Joe started it with little noise, and using no lights, eased the bus out of the garage. The vehicles of those days carried no backup lights, otherwise the boss might have seen us. He failed to hear us too; at least his room remained dark when we left the garage and drove north.

Joe drove about two hundred yards before coming to the asphalt road. There he turned on the headlights and aimed the bus toward Peachers Mill Pike. After we had traveled a couple of miles on the pike, Fleming asked for his turn at the wheel. What great fun — I could see myself in the driver's seat.

Before pulling to the roadside and stopping the bus on a hill, Joe had driven us beyond the first crossing of North Fork Creek, the stream that meanders through Garretts. Fleming moved to the driver's seat and touched the starter button with his toe. The engine failed to start — it didn't even turn over. He tried again, and then again. With each attempt, the successively lower tones said that the bus had no intention of starting.

Joe moved up to the driver seat, saying,

"Here, let me try it."

He turned the headlights off and stepped on the starter button. With the battery power almost spent, the starter grunted to dead stop.

"What are we going to do?" I asked anxiously.

"We're in a lot of trouble if we leave the bus here."

Without saying another word, Joe stepped out on the road, opened the hood and looked at the engine. Fleming and I followed

"We can go to the barn, bring the tractor and tow it back," Fleming suggested.

This sounded like a good plan. Fleming and I would walk to the dairy barn and return with the tractor. Meanwhile, Joe would stay with the bus and try to start the engine.

From where we had stopped, the most direct route to the barn would take us through Garretts. We climbed the fence and moved toward the dark woods. After hiking a short distance and working our way into the dense brush thicket, I said,

"Fleming, we could have saved time if we had gone by the road."

"We've already started now so let's keep going. It's a lot less distance this way."

As we dug our way through a heavy brush, Fleming bent the branches forward and released them with a swish. I tried to shield myself with my arms. Although the limbs smacked me in the face and chest, I preferred to suffer the torture than to fall behind. Little light filtered through the trees from the star-filled sky. We half stumbled down a steep descent that we knew as First Hill.

Suddenly, a night creature dashed off through the underbrush — at least, that's what it sounded like. The darkness kept us from seeing the thing. Apparently, the critter had dashed away from us out of fear, but fear ran in both directions. With unsure footing, we made our way down the steep hill.

Soon a softly muffled rumble arose and surrounded us in the darkness. Louder than the noises our footsteps made, the sounds of thumps and gushing water seemed to intensify. Thump-swish, thump-swish, thump-swish, the puzzling noise seemed to become louder with each step. Whatever it was, we were walking toward it. Without slowing, Fleming continued his push through the brush and the black night. I followed. My heart pounded at double the rhythm of the mysterious thumps, and almost as loud.

Breaking the silence at last, Fleming asked,

"Do you hear that noise?"

My anxiety eased at once, just knowing that, he too, heard the pounding. He solved the puzzle before I could answer.

"That's the ram pump at the First Hill spring."

I breathed easier — I had heard those sounds before. The village of New Providence pumped its water from the spring.

A few minutes later, we reached the bottom of the hill, left the woods and crossed the snake-filled creek. We still had another mile to go. A dirt road and the dim light of the stars made traveling the remaining distance easier. Nearly an hour had passed from the time we had climbed the Garretts fence and arrived at the dairy barn.

Even in the cold weather, the tractor started with ease. We traveled at low speed until we reached a safe distance from the main building. The tractor carried no lights, but a flashlight we found at the dairy barn helped guide us. When we arrived on Peachers Mill Pike, Joe was shivering inside the bus.

We chained the tractor to the bumper and began the slow return trip. Arriving with the bus in tow, we again throttled the tractor to a low speed as we neared the garage. I unhooked the bus and we pushed it back into its parking place. We returned the tractor to the barn hours after we had driven away in the bus.

The next morning at the breakfast table no one noticed the three sleepy boys. As we filed out of the dining hall, Mr. Acree said to Joe,

"Before you bring the school bus around this morning, be sure you fill the radiator. Last night I drained the water, thinking it might freeze and crack the motor."

So that was the problem. The bone-dry engine had simply overheated and locked up. I had failed to get a turn at driving the bus, but the hike through the pitch-dark woods of Garretts would be a night to remember. Our bus trip to nowhere remained a secret.

We stuck together, mostly against the boss, but also against those from the outside. The orphanage boys were brothers in the larger sense, but we all learned to love success and hate defeat. A spirit of strife marked all our sports efforts, as we were rivals in our games. Later, when playing high school football, I would use the aggressive drive learned in these childhood sports. We played with a fixed idea of winning.

The triumphs on the baseball field gave our boys a deep pride in our teams. For years, orphanage played other clubs from throughout the area. By the time I was old enough to make the team, however, all this had changed. There were not enough boys left to field a team. With the young men going off to war, sports fell from the spotlight.

I was six to eight years old during the heyday of our winning teams. Even later, I was too young to make the team. That turned me off to the sport. Besides, an older boy or sometimes Mr. Acree, would often give me a task that further swayed me against the game.

"Buddy, you go over and stand beyond the fence in right field and throw the ball back, in case someone hits it there."

Baseball, I thought as I stood waiting, should offer more than my returning a ball knocked over the fence. This assigned chore, along with my failure to make the team, caused me to loose interest. Even if it is America's most loved sport, I formed a lasting distaste for baseball.

Football was different. As a youngster, I loved to play the game of touch. After we decided to choose sides for a game, a boy would throw a stick or bat into the air. His opponent, and leader of the other team, caught it at midpoint and held it in a vertical position. The first boy then grasped the bat as the second boy let go. They alternated, hand over hand, until they reached the top.

The one who was last able to grasp bat without letting it drop started the choosing process. He chose the best player first. The team leaders continued to choose until they had picked every boy who wanted to join the game. The system yielded evenly matched baseball and football teams.

During the later years, after Mr. Acree had left the orphanage, there weren't enough boys to have a game of football. On Sunday afternoons we walked to the school grounds in New Providence. There we found enough willing players.

We played touch football with vigor, most of the time using the two-hand tag rules. Instead of tackling a boy who carried the ball, we needed only to touch him with both hands. The players were to block, block and block. As we used neither helmets nor safety pads in playing this sand-lot football, I count myself lucky to have come through unscathed. It's a wonder we survived the rough-neck game.

We at the orphanage played hard, as if we had something to prove. Most of the boys shared this attitude at fun time — victory meant all. That was a virtue to which we all aspired. The corporate spirit demanded it — we simply had to excel.

Chapter 11
School Days

The Orphanage School

I turned six years old and the first day of school came and went, but there was no straining of a child-parent bond. There was no bawling, no fear of a strange new building. Neither anxiety nor surprise attended this milestone of life — I cannot even recall that first day of school.

Most first-time students leave home and travel to another place to attend school, but not the boys and girls at the orphanage. The boys' dorm and school were in the same building. We simply descended one flight of stairs and entered the classroom. The girls needed to walk from the main building, less than a hundred yards away.

Our grammar school took up most of the first floor in the structure that we called the boys' building. An entrance hall ran between the classrooms on one side and the auditorium on the other. The assembly room had 160 seats. A crowd of 200 people fit into the room with the aisles lined with extra chairs.

Education at the orphanage was a very important business; the school season ran 5 days a week for 10 months of the year. School ran from eight until mid-afternoon, with a break for lunch. The teachers and the students returned to the classroom after supper. This formal homework session, which we called study hall, carried as much weight as the daytime classes.

Mrs. Kate McDaniel, who lived near within sight, taught the higher grades. Mrs. Frances Hambaugh taught the first through fourth grades. She lived in New Providence, about a half mile from the orphanage. A lady in her mid-to-late thirties, Miss Frances wore her long brown hair pulled back. She had a beautiful round face. By her kindness, her gentle manner and her soft and friendly voice, she earned my lasting respect. This super teacher's love and tenderness were like the sunbeams that pop out at the end of a summer shower. It's little wonder that all the children seemed to admire her more than the other adults who had authority over us. Miss Frances gained this status because she showed a basic respect for each boy and girl — making us feel like individuals instead of objects.

I was six years old in 1932 and the only child in the orphanage to start the first grade. There was no kindergarten. I hoped to move up to the second grade the next fall, but Miss Frances had a different plan. She said,

"Buddy, you will have company in the first grade this year."

Did she say first grade? The news surprised and baffled me. She gently told me that I was to repeat the grade. The news crushed me, but I failed to ask her to explain.

I wondered why. Did I have a learning problem? No! Did my stubborn streak show its face in the school room? I was seven, but this aspect of my family genes had yet to appear.

She held me back because there would have been no other second grade students that fall. My presence in the first grade swelled the class to three students. The third student lived on an adjoining farm and entered the orphanage's school. Miss Frances, in using the one-room-school method of teaching, needed more than a single person in each grade. Mary Frances Williams and I were the two resident members of the second grade in 1935.

We remained classmates through the seventh grade — that is, until the school closed, and we started at New Providence. The third person moved away later, but Mary Frances and I would complete high school in the class of 1947.

In those early years, our teacher used methods that made learning easy. Miss Frances would start the other grades on their studies and then call a class to the front bench. For example, she may have asked the first graders to copy the letters she'd written in the blackboard. We used a chalk board, a piece of black slate, nine by twelve inches, enclosed in a wooden frame. Since there were more than one class in the same room, we soon learned what the higher grades studied. Before I had reached third grade, I knew that the multiplication tables were very important. I had heard the class drills many times.

One day, during second grade, the class sat at the front bench and Miss Frances said

"Buddy, don't just sit there. You should practice writing the letters that I'm writing on the board."

Although she had told us to write, I had stopped. Even so, the comment surprised me. Miss Frances had spoken without turning away from her writing on the blackboard. Somehow, she knew that I wasn't writing; but how? Were the rumors true — does she have eyes in the back of her head?

She Has Eyes in the Back of Her Head?

I searched long and hard for concealed eyes, but saw nothing more than her brown hair pulled into a tight bun. This puzzled me until about two years later when she had asked several boys to her home for cookies. I recalled for her the event that still baffled me, and asked,

"How did you know without even turning away from the blackboard that I wasn't writing?"

"When I didn't hear the chalk scratching on the slate, I knew that you weren't doing the practice writing."

We learned more than the basic three R's in Miss France's schoolroom. The sessions I liked the most were those times she read aloud from the Bible. The story of Jonah stuck in the whale's belly, of Delilah trimming Samson's hair, and the parting of the Red Sea as the Israelite's escaped from Egypt, inspired me. I loved these narratives. At the expense of my own school work, I often eavesdropped as she read to, or taught, the other grades.

As Miss Frances read the drama-filled stories, I imagined myself as King David of old. David was my name and my daydreams seemed real. I walked into the valley to do battle with Goliath. This Bible story prompted me, like my namesake, to make a sling of leather strips. I practiced tossing stones for many hours. My aim improved — I often hit the target tree or banged a tin can off the fence post.

From the fourth grade on, I recall only a few of the details that seem hidden within a haze, but one view is clear: I couldn't wait to grow up. There I sat, stuck in grade school going nowhere. The long days in class slowly dragged by. From my desk, I gazed out the window for seemingly endless hours. Lost in the grip of my daydreams, I tried to escape the boring present.

A morning shadow fell on the boiler's roof from the girls' dorm and slowly marched across the tin. I followed the shade, crease by crease, and counted the minutes. Although I pushed harder and harder on the accelerator of time's engine, it seemed to grind slower and slower. I craved speed through those long days of the fifth, sixth and seventh grades, but time's motor droned on at its painfully slow pace. It seemed that I would never escape from this stage of my life.

The local School Board paid the teachers at the orphanage. The board also paid the orphanage a small rental fee for the use of classrooms. This allowed the four or five children who lived nearby to attend our school.

Mrs. Kate, who taught the fifth through eighth grades, passed away in 1939, leaving Miss Frances as the orphanage's only teacher. The next year, our school moved from the boys' building to the unused nursery in the main building. I was in the fifth grade. By 1942, the head count had dwindled to less than twenty pupils, including those from the outside. With too few students to warrant holding classes, the school closed.

New Providence Grade School

I entered public school for the first time in 1942 as a fourteen-year-old eighth grade student. My older sister, June, had started high school one year before. My sister Barbara, brother Fred and I joined the other children and hiked a bit more than a mile to the New Providence School.

Until I moved into my teen years, the superintendents had looked inward. They believed that our mixing with boys and girls from the outside would somehow leave a bad effect. The children who lived on the nearby farms and attended our school were exempt from this rule. Of course, the older students could associate with their classmates at Clarksville High.

When starting grade school at New Providence, we began to mix with outside children. Mr. Acree had left by then.

We welcomed this rule change offered by the new superintendent. It opened new doors and gave us greater freedom. I gladly engaged in the school functions and even took a bit role in the eighth grade play. This meant my staying after class to practice. On Sunday afternoons, we often walked to the public school grounds and played sports with the local boys.

We made friends. They often asked us to visit their homes, but we didn't ask them to visit us. I met Mack Johnson at the school. He would marry my sister Barbara less than a year after they graduated from high school. Mack chummed around with three boys from the orphanage — Ben, Fred and me. A few other local boys joined our circle to start a troop of boy scouts, but we had neither a sponsor nor a scoutmaster. I had been a member for a few months until our leader left to join the army.

I was older and held the rank of second class scout — one step above the lowest grade — so the others made me the acting leader. The group operated in an easy-going manner that would fail to meet the standards of a normal troop. Our projects did not qualify as scout programs.

Once day we planned to cook a chicken. We trekked to a wooded area by the Cumberland River where I removed the hen from the bag and wrung its neck. From that point on we strayed from the usual means of cooking, for we had brought no cooking utensils. Instead of immersing the bird in boiling water and plucking its feathers, we skinned it. We gathered wood, started a fire and roasted the chicken for two hours. Still, it was too raw to eat. Of course, we failed to earn a Boy Scout cooking merit badge.

Future teachers learned some special crafts at the New Providence School. They would need the skills to teach in the rural areas of Tennessee. This teacher-training goal brought a novel curriculum to the school. Each spring the students planted a large vegetable garden on the grounds. This project carried a great value due to the war effort — it helped to train the school children and the future teachers.

I felt a sense of pride that we at the orphanage already knew how to plant and care for a vegetable garden. Many families "ate out of a paper bag." This described the people who brought their food at a store and brought it home in a paper bag. They consumed food that some other person had grown. This term and "Victory Garden" came into use during the war when so much of the country's food went to feed the military. We at the orphanage wanted to help the war effort by growing food. Many of our "brothers" served in the Army, Navy, Marines and Air Corps.

The school children showed great interest in the projects that helped the war effort. One task involved the collection of scrap metal. The school classes broke up into rival teams and tried to outdo each other by gathering the most scrap. Our efforts at this not only served a good purpose — it also helped put a bit of money in my pockets.

A number of wrought iron fences fell victim to the war and vanished from the area. Scraps of rusted metal seemed to hide in the weeds near our barn where we stored the farm tools. Our search for cast-iron led us to comb the area. It brought a premium of ten cents per pound, while sheet metal sold for less than half that rate. Other metals such as brass and copper brought an even better price. The activity meant big money to us.

On a Saturday we would yoke the team of oxen, load the wagon with scrap metal and deliver it to Lui Hiemanshon. This local scrap dealer's business was in Clarksville on a hill high above the river. More than once, the oxen strained under a heavy load, at times going down on their knees to nudge the wagon up the steep incline.

Mr. Hiemanshon wrote a ticket and gave us a check in payment for each load. Before handing over the check, he read aloud the amount written on the check and then repeated it several times. After going through this routine he handed over the check and ticket, saying,

"Young man, this check for five dollars and thirty-four cents is big money."

The school principal, relying on the bill of sale given with each delivery, judged which group had gathered the most scrap iron. This competition at school helped direct many loads of scarce metal to the nation's war machine.

During recess one day, several boys were pitching horseshoes. Mr. Wright, our eighth grade teacher, rushed around the corner of the school building and shouted,

"Okay, all you boys who are shooting dice will stay after school."

What was he talking about? No one was shooting dice!

"We were pitching horseshoes, not shooting dice," we said in almost one voice.

"You all are staying after school."

Our protests failed to convince the teacher that we had not been gambling. He must have based his reaction on a single remark he'd overheard. It seems that one boy, insisting on his turn to pitch, said

"It's my shot next."

From where he stood, out of sight, beyond the corner of the building, Mr. Wright overheard the remark. He wrongly assumed that we were shooting dice. After school that day, several boys grumbled in low tones about the false charges.

In spite of this event, I enjoyed going to school in New Providence. We saw many interesting things on our daily walks to and from school. Only two blocks west of the orphanage was a large tobacco warehouse. From our vantage point on the street we watched workmen inside the building. Using a large press, they packed bundles of tobacco leaves into giant wooden casks. Loaded and packed, these eight foot diameter hogsheads were from three up to six feet high. The workers turned the hogsheads up and rolled them onto the waiting trucks.

Our duties at the orphanage came first, but the school also had projects. One school task, my acting as a crossing guard, took some time after classes. The school system had no paid crossing guards in those days, so the eighth-grade teacher asked a student to act the part. Armed with a bright-orange shoulder belt and a red flag tied to a fishing pole, I headed to Highway 41W fifteen minutes before the classes ended. There I stopped the cars and trucks to help the lower-grade students cross the busy road.

A boy charged with a daily task needed a good reason to be late, for the boss expected him to come home promptly after school. This rule, of course, applied to Fred — he worked in the dairy. Each day, he missed the after-school fun. Instead, he headed to Garretts to bring the cows to the dairy barn. His milking the cows came before everything else. On most days, my kitchen-boy job required that I show up thirty minutes before supper.

Another reason to stay after school came near the end of the school year, in the spring of 1943. I landed my first paying job. Near the end of the school year, the principal Dr. D. Harley Fite, called me in his office.

"Would you like to earn a little money?"

"Yes sir, I would," I answered.

He told me to collect the bean poles from the garden so the teachers could use them the next year. I was to clear the vegetation from the garden plot and the dead bean plants from the poles. He paid me fifteen cents per hour. This was big money, for in those days five cents bought a large candy bar. With part of the earnings, I started my first bank savings account.

Clarksville High School

High school differed from grade school in several ways. First, we walked less — only three blocks to the highway where we caught the bus. Along with the other students living nearby, the five or six residents of the orphanage rode the public school bus to

Clarksville High. (Mr. Widgery had sold the bus.) Second, the class format changed.

Mary Frances Williams and I, along with about 100 students from other county grade schools, entered the 1943 freshman class. Many of the teachers had taught boys and girls from the orphanage. My sister June moved into the junior class that year. Barbara would start high school one year later, and Fred a year after that.

The high school day started under the watchful eye of our homeroom teacher, and then we moved room to room throughout the day according to the subjects taken. Miss Marie Riggins, an English teacher, was my homeroom teacher for the entire four years. She also taught me how to conjugate verbs. Ever-erect, her bearing bespoke the strict style she used in dealing with students.

The day began with roll call and announcements. After this session that lasted ten minutes, we headed to the first period class. The school day broke into class sessions of 55 minutes plus a 45 minute break for lunch. A period for study hall allowed us to work on the assigned lessons.

At midterm of the freshman year I held an enviable attendance record. I had not missed a single day of school from the start. That good record was about to end. One morning I overheard two boys talking on the school bus. The topic tweaked my interest, so I joined the discourse.

Sunny, a boy from New Providence, knew of a cave in the high bluff that overlooked the Cumberland River. This was the first I'd heard of it. Sunny needed a partner to help explore the site, but the plan involved some danger. The venture might offer a chance for a great thrill, so I agreed to go with him. Instead of heading to our homerooms upon arriving at school that morning, we hitchhiked the five miles back to Sonny's home in New Providence. We needed to get some items crucial to the trip.

With the rope, flashlight and our lunches in hand, we headed across the Darnell farm toward the river. The rope would allow us to drop down from the cliff top, the only way to reach the cave's entrance. Less than an hour after leaving Sonny's home we arrived at the bluff above the Cumberland River. Sonny tied the rope to a tree. We carefully lowered ourselves down the jagged stone wall and landed on a ledge at the small cave's mouth.

We were hungry by then, so before entering the hole in the rocks we decided to open our brown paper bags. We ate lunch near the cave and enjoyed the scenic view of the lowlands across the river. Our feet dangled over the ledge.

Smoke had charred the ceiling near the cave's entrance. A frame of loose stones outlined a fire box, telling us that we weren't the first to visit the site. Dust covered the remains of a blaze from earlier times. Narrow crevices prevented our going more than a few yards into the cave. That was okay, for the chattering and fluttering noises indicated that bats lived in the deeper furrows.

When we came out of the cave it was raining, so we sat beneath the overhung lip and waited. We planned to leave as soon as it stopped raining. Using the rope again, we climbed the steep, and now wet, rocks of the cliff.

The day had passed quickly. Walking fast, I covered the distance back to the bus stop in a much shorter time than it had taken to go the other way. I wanted to arrive with the others, or Superintendent Kilpatrick might wonder why I failed to come home. As it turned out, it would not have mattered. The boss already knew of my truancy, but he did not say a word to me about it. Maybe he didn't want a confrontation — he was to leave soon.

It seems that Miss Riggins had asked the other riders if I had been on the bus that morning. She passed the news to the principal, for I was absent from class without a reason.

The next morning, I walked into the classroom before the bell rang. Miss Riggins said,

"David, you're to go to the principal's office at once."

On the way down the hall, I knew that I had made a big mistake. Until that moment, I had given little regard to what might result from my having played hooky.

With head bowed, I walked into the office. Instead of his usual dark suite that morning, Mr. Howard stood there in shirt sleeves. A heavy-set man, he wore both a belt and suspenders. Glaring at me from behind the nearly chest-high counter, his posture seemed to ask, "Why did you let me down?" He did not ask for an explanation.

The stern look soon vanished from his face, and he said gently,

"Until now David, your deportment has been good, so I'm giving you a light penalty. I'm going to cut your grade by five points on each subject, but if you ever skip school again we'll make it a lot harder on you. Now, return to your homeroom."

I wanted to make good grades — so the punishment did hurt. Miss Riggins showed a soft side not evident until this incident. After the five-point penalty, she scored me with a 90 in her English class. Miss Riggins was the strictest teacher in high school, but my view of her soared when she handed me that next report card.

Toward the end of the first year, I stopped by Mrs. Lester Page's Latin classroom. A short matronly woman, she often wore her hair in a knot pulled behind her head. I told her that I wanted to become a Latin student the following year. She nearly floored me with her response.

Mrs. Page said:

"Latin is a dead language; It has value for the person who plans to go on to college. Since you're not, you don't need to take Latin."

"Latin is a dead language," she said. "It only has value for the person who plans to go on to college. Since you're not, you don't need to take Latin." She continued without pause: "You should make better use of your time in high school. I suggest you take something that involves working with your hands like manual training."

It irritated me that she saw my future in such limited terms. I thought back to that hot day, some two years into the past. I was at work shocking corn. The beads of salty sweat burned the cuts and scratches on my arms, adding to the pain as I worked. I silently recalled, and again affirmed, the goals I'd set for myself that day. I would not be a farmer. Mrs. Page could not hear the voice inside me shouting — "I will, I will go to college!"

I didn't tell her about my dream, about my goal. It made no difference if I took Latin or not, the dream would not end, even if it meant a struggle.

The next year, instead of studying Latin, I took a class in wood working. The term project was to built a footstool. The encouragement that Mr. Howard, Miss Riggins and the football coaches gave me more than made up for the remarks by Mrs. Page. Despite her remarks I took a course of math and science that I might gain an engineering base. I focused on football as well as scholarship.

Boys from the orphanage had excelled in high school sports over the years. During one season in the 1930s, seven of our boys were on the school's starting baseball team.

Howard (Smiley) Johnson, one of our young men, earned a chance to play football at University of Georgia. After a stellar career there, the Green Bay Packers offered him a contract. He played one season of pro football, until World War II came and he joined the Marines. Captain Howard Johnson, like thousands of other young men, lost his life on a small island called Iwo Jima. Many heroes sprang from our own ranks. Some of our idols were in the service, others were first-rate athletes and some were both.

With the success of my forerunners, I always knew that I would go out for football. Everyone at the orphanage expected me to do well. These facts gave me heart, but two things troubled me — my weight and my slowness. I weighed only 150 pounds, light for a football player. As for speed, I could outrun only two of all the boys who tried out for the team. I hoped to excel on the gridiron, but somehow I needed to compensate for these two drawbacks.

At the start of the second year, I resolved to block and tackle during practice as if we were in a game with Springfield, our biggest rival. This plan of endless hard-nosed action worked — Coach Cecil soon noticed the change and asked me to work out with the varsity team. He let me play in the next game, and I soon earned a slot on the first, or starting, team.

I found success on the gridiron, but it had little to do with the sport of football. In a sense, the actions of certain other students propelled me. They clustered in close-knit bunches and shunned all outsiders. Maybe it was cultural shock on my part, but this behavior didn't make sense. Life at the orphanage had not prepared me for the social life of teen-age cliques. I viewed these acts as a personal snub, thinking they might have stemmed from where I lived.

We lived on an equal social plane at the orphanage, as does any large family. If a person acted as if he were better than the others, someone brought him down to size. When these students turned their backs on me physically as well as figuratively, it hurt. I had to respond — I had to belong. That was basic.

Success at football would serve as my leverage to become somebody. I had to prove a point, to open doors, to earn the acceptance I so craved. Making the team was the most important thing in my life.

My distress ended only after it became clear that the classmates weren't shunning me. I later sensed that many of them acted the way they did because, like me, they were insecure teens. Those bad feelings, however, helped me win a starting slot on the varsity team under Coach Cecil. The next year, Mr. Frank Ditmore took the job as head coach. He challenged us to think "winning" full time.

> ## Coach Ditmore said:
> "If you want to win at football, you must eat, sleep and live the game full time."

"If you want to win at football, you must eat, sleep and live the game."

Football occupied a big place in my mind, both in and out of season. This staunch mind-set clashed with my life at the orphanage a few times.

One day in the fall, soon after the start of school, Mr. Widgery told me to come home on the bus instead of staying for practice. A field of corn was ready for harvest. To him, the work was more important than football, but not to me. After school that day, instead of taking to the field with the team, I picked corn. The angry frustrations inside me exploded. I threw the corn at the wagon with all my strength. Missing practice was a serious matter, but the coach seemed to accept my excuse.

A short time after he took over, Coach Ditmore saddled me with a nickname. He was first to observe, or at least first to remark about, the change in my appearance. I allowed my sideburns to grow down below my ears for one reason only, that was to look unique. I was the only student to adopt the look that had been in vogue almost a hundred years earlier. Elvis Presley would revive the hair style some twenty years later.

My long sideburns caused the desired result — I received the attention. The coach dubbed me "Honest Abe."

Soon, the football players and other students shortened the name to "Abe." The name stuck with the high school crowd. The people at the orphanage still called me "Buddy," as they had done since I was six.

I simply was doing the same thing that today's teens do. I wore the hair style or dressed for no other reason than to draw attention. This chapter in my background allows me to relate to the aims of teenage boys and girls. Their spiked hair, outlandish clothing and other tricks of image making seem to shout, "Look at me — I'm somebody."

I've been there — I understand the motive. My long sideburns, as well as my drive to succeed on the football field, served this purpose. These rituals earned me a measure of social acceptance.

My teammates chose me to captain the team for the senior year of 1946-47. The Clarksville High School football team had its most successful seasons ever during my junior and senior years. These teams put together a string of twenty games without a loss. This record rated us among the best in Tennessee and brought an invitation to a post-season game in Mississippi. That state's best team, McComb High School, had not allowed a score. Playing in the Memorial Bowl at Jackson, we made one touchdown, but they made three and handily beat us.

Many of the football players excelled in education as well as we did on the sports field. Nine of the boys on the starting team made the National Honor Society. The single day of my truancy, during the freshman year, helped me focus on good grades. That incident, thanks to the five-point grade loss that Mr. Howard dished out, shocked me into a healthy respect for the learning process. Hard work was the only way to make good grades.

I recalled the study habits we used in grade school. There, we engaged in an hour of formal study each night under the watchful eyes of Miss Frances. She told us,

"Even if you have done the assigned work, read forward into the next lesson. Learning will come easier when we get to it in class."

I returned to these study habits, and set aside one hour to engage in the homework. I often did the homework at school, but still set aside the hour between seven and eight o'clock. After that, I was free to catch my choice radio programs.

I favored a show called "Mr. District Attorney." It aired Wednesday nights at eight. We enjoyed programs such as "Amos and Andy, Fibber Magee and Molly, and The Shadow." These radio dramas of the 1930's and 40's allowed me to enjoy many flights of fancy.

My having set a fixed time for daily study paid off in a big way. The good grades allowed me to join both the National Athletic Scholastic Society and the National Honor Society. High school had become a pleasant place by the second year. My classmates seemed to accept me for who I was, and not as a person from the orphanage. I made many friends who had the same interests. Football was only one of these.

The students elected me class president for our junior year, a job that offered me some useful lessons. I learned to stand before a group without having my knees knock together. The next year, a few friends insisted that I seek the presidency of the student body. I did, but in a close election lost the race. This worked to my advantage.

Before the start of school that next fall, the vice-president elect and his family moved away. A special election of the student body gave me the office. I chaired the student council, a group of members chosen by each homeroom. This duty put me in close contact with the teachers and school officials, where I gained many skills such as dealing with people. This office, along with some good grades, helped me win a trip sponsored by a local civic club. Volunteer Boys State was the name of this week of fun and learning about politics.

The last year of high school passed on favorable terms. By serving as the team captain during the best-ever season, I had topped my wildest hopes. In 1946 the Joy Jewelry Company started giving an annual award to the best football player. I won the Joy

Award that year, a gold watch with twenty-one jewels. During that last football practice in the spring, I helped coach the junior varsity team. My brother Fred was in the group.

Each spring, the senior students voted for the class superlatives and reported the results in the yearbook. They honored me with three awards: the most courteous boy, the best boy citizen, and the boy most likely to succeed.

The teachers voted me the best all-around senior for the 1946-47 school year. With this, the school officials asked me to say a few words at the graduation ceremony. In a speech written by the teacher-advisor, I gave an outline of the schooling our class had received.

Two of us from the orphanage graduated that spring. Among the class total of 172, there were 91 girls and 81 boys. Thirty-one young men, in the wake of their wartime military service, had returned to finish high school with the class of 1947.

Finally, this last day, which often seemed as if it would never come, did arrive. It marked the end of my long stay at the orphanage. With a major in science and math, I set my sights on college. In spite of Mrs. Page's prediction, I looked forward to college life in Knoxville. The University of Tennessee there had accepted me as a student.

Chapter 12
Looking Ahead

Every other boy in the dorm slept soundly, but I lay awake tossing in the bed. I turned the pillow over to find a cool spot. A hot breeze carried the noise of a large truck engine straining under a heavy load on Highway 41W. The driver double-clutched the vehicle as it crawled out of the river valley along the steep hill. These sounds, piercing the quiet night, invited me to enter a realm of fancy. In my mind's eye, I was in the truck's cab riding to wherever the highway led — destination didn't matter.

When a youngster, these thoughts often crossed my mind. Many times a train's whistle, blasting its hauntingly forlorn tones deep into the night, skipped across the mile of the hilly countryside to shatter the silence. The sounds summoned me aboard the train. Mixing hope with a flight of fancy, my youthful mind ran the iron rails with the click-clack of the speeding wheels.

I imagined what it would be like to ride in a Pullman car as the train carried me further and further away. The act of leaving, not a final stop, was important. Any other place would be better than the orphanage as I slowly passed through the ninth to twelfth years. That "other place" existed only in a dream.

These wishful thoughts of travel magnified a wish to escape from the status quo of orphanage life. I felt caged. The dreams arose out of a suppressed rage and unhappy state of mind. I nursed those feelings, on and off, from the time we arrived until a spirit of hope came along to banish the mood despair.

This dark mood ruled my thoughts through the early years at the orphanage, and only abated as I approached the mid-teen years. The change began that day in the corn field when I glimpsed a vision of the future and decided never to become a farmer.

My spirits soared on the day Mr. Acree retired. A bit-by-bit progress carried through the terms of Superintendents Widgery and Kilpatrick.

Perhaps the move toward maturity had something to do with this new outlook. Still, as I grew into the normal phase of puberty life, some harsh problems troubled me. Often becoming upset and irritable without cause — my moods changed as often as the wind. I could not understand why. Something strange was happening to me at this point, but what? Why did my thoughts often turn upside down?

Much of the torment came from ignorance. I had no idea that every young man goes through these body changes. Without a source of helpful facts, I simply mulled through those gloomy, up-and-down mood swings. I needed the benefit of adult counsel, but lived through this stage before learning the facts. Even a little knowledge about this normal process could have helped to ease the distress.

After passing the troubled teen years, I struggled with fewer inner conflicts. I spent more time thinking about the direction of my life. The new outlook replaced the feeling of self-pity that had stalked me for years. Heartened by the new way Mr. Byrom ran the orphanage, this fresh mood began to ease the pain I had suffered during those early years. With added purpose, I refined and honed the guideposts I had set in the early teens. Hoping to avoid a life of hard labor, I would use brain power instead of brawn power. With a bit of luck, plus the added drive on my part, I could make it.

Building on the past, I slowly came to terms with my status as a resident of the orphanage. A calmer temper replaced the tense and vexing feelings of the earlier days. I still had a few problems, but they faded as I found answers to the questions that every teenage boy faces:

"How should I react with my peers? With girls? How can I best work toward the goals I'd set? How does all this fit into my plans for a future career?"

All I had endured at the orphanage had helped to form the new outlook. The bad memories of those first several years did not go away, but I refused to dwell on them. Current interests called for new ways of looking at things. I saw the difference between the road to a bright future and the dull life I hoped to avoid. I also knew that times had to get better, as they already had. The lessons learned during my life in the orphanage helped in a number of ways.

I learned to assume the responsibility of a given task. Mr. Acree always followed through, making sure that each child completed the chore he assigned. Dating back to my first assigned duty, that of keeping the lawn clean, he made a special effort to check my work. The same applied to my kitchen-boy duties. Both jobs were high-profile tasks. Mr. Acree taught a "Will to work" that stayed with me after he left and I took on the more important jobs. One of these chores was to fix the broken machines.

The mechanical nature of this work taught me to think in a logical manner. One idea along this line had come to me when I was about ten years old. The theme whirled through my mind for many months and led me to dream about a special device.

I planned to design and build a perpetual motion machine. Although I had heard such a machine was impossible to built, it didn't stop me from claiming that it was feasible — I knew how.

The plan was simple. To start, I would hook a generator to one shaft of an electric motor that had shafts coming from both sides. I would then start the motor using power from the house electric outlet. A special switch controlled the machine. Once it ran at full speed, this switch would shut down the house current and take power from the generator. This newly generated power would drive the machine.

Only the starter power was to come from the house outlet; the energy from the generator would take over. Useful work would come from the motor's other shaft. Presto — we have free power.

Wild enthusiasm about the plan hummed through my mind. I felt that I had something big and wouldn't let the idea die. I shared these thoughts with several older boys, but received little backing. They seemed to lose interest as soon as I said perpetual motion machine.

Finally, the boy in charge of the plumbing shop tired of my persistence and set out to prove the flaw in my idea. He said,

"Think about this Buddy, can you push a wagon that's going faster than you can run?"

"No."

"Well, your machine is like that. The motor cannot run fast enough to furnish the power needed to run the generator. Your motor needs to run faster than the generator and the generator needs to run faster than the motor."

Continuing, he foretold what would happen if we tested the idea,

"If you build and start such a rig, its speed will gradually slow and then stop. It would never do any useful work."

The plan died a slow death in spite of the obvious flaws. The logic of his words, however, did persuade me to drop the idea for making a model.

As did each boy, I too, grew into bigger jobs that matched my size and talents. If we had a problem with electric wiring or water pipes, we fixed the fault ourselves instead of calling a service man.

The older boys did a number of special jobs such as shoe repair, dairy farming and plumbing. Many former residents can trace their life's work to the skills they gained from the chores assigned them. After leaving the orphanage, many of them started a plumbing, electric or farming business.

During those last few years, as number of residents dwindled, I was the oldest boy. Several tasks came with this new status. One included repairing farm machines and another involved making electrical repairs. During World War II and later, we repaired machines, using patched instead of new parts. We had to make do with the materials at hand.

Superintendent Byrom owned an old Plymouth that had quit running. I persuaded him to let me repair it, if we could find the needed parts. After we located a set of piston rings and crankcase bushings, he okayed the attempt.

I had never tried to overhaul an engine, but began by taking the motor apart without removing it from the car. The job took two days, after which the engine started on the first try. What a thrill! Mr. Byrom praised the work and said that I would make a good mechanical engineer. His remarks helped me decide to study engineering.

I enjoyed the challenge of trying to figure out how things worked. Many times, I took a device apart for no other reason than to satisfy a whim — to see how it worked. Sometimes a machine failed to work when I put it back together, but that didn't stop my experiments.

Tinkering was fun. This convinced me that if I could only learn how a machine worked, I could fix anything. By the time Mr.

Byrom arrived, I did most of the electrical repairs. A hot wire didn't scare me, but after several shocks, I gained a healthy respect for it. Besides this electrical work, I fixed leaky water pipes and did other service jobs around the orphanage as the need arose.

Someone had to do these tasks. Even though I often didn't know how to solve a problem, I made the effort. Given the wartime parts problems, we learned to conserve. We reused old electric wire, threaded and installed rusted water pipes or welded the broken machine parts. This phase lasted two or three years. It helped to confirm my desire to become an engineer, but should I pursue, electrical or mechanical?

I would decide later. Machine parts, I could see and touch, but not electrons, so I set my sights on a degree in mechanical engineering. This work experience helped to form a life plan. The high school counselor gave me a battery of tests. The results implied that two prospects would best match my talents. I would do well to work with mechanical things, or with people.

To reach a goal of becoming an engineer, I had to attend college. A lack of funds would be a serious problem. The only way I could expect to make it was to earn enough money to pay my own way. Going to college would not be easy, but I knew that would be my only way of avoiding making a living by hard labor.

Mr. Byrom both encouraged and expressed faith in me with words such as,

"You can do it. All you need is a strong determination. You can do anything that you set your mind to."

I believed him. His emotional support and positive attitude inspired me, but Mr. Byrom did more than simply cheer me from the sideline.

He helped arrange the means by which I might start earning the needed finances by giving me a pig. He took piglets from a newly weaned sow and gave one to each boy in the sixth grade or higher. I was elated when he told us,

"The animal belongs to you, and only to you. We will supply the feed, but you must look after it, so remember one thing — They're your pigs."

I had saved a small sum of money, dating back to the fifteen-cents per hour job given me by Dr. Fite, head of New Providence

School. In addition, the scrap iron I had collected and sold helped my savings account as much as it helped the war effort. Other funds had come from our digging the may-apple roots at Garretts. Drug companies used these plants to make some kind of medicine, so the scrap dealer readily offered us cash for our produce. I had saved nearly fifty dollars by the time Mr. Byrom gave me the piglet.

The female animal matured and produced a litter of eight. I sold the sow and brood of pigs. With the proceeds, I bought a young calf. Later, just before leaving the orphanage, I sold the steer. This swelled the bank account to nearly three hundred dollars.

I had applied to the University of Tennessee, Knoxville. Since I had made good grades in high school, they accepted me. I had kept in touch with Mother, and planned to live with her after leaving the orphanage. Her apartment was within walking distance of the college campus.

After she finished school at Fort Sanders Hospital, Mother worked as a private duty nurse. A few years later she returned to work at the hospital. With the start of World War II, she took a job as an industrial nurse with the Aluminum Company of America. She still worked there In 1947 when I finished high school.

A family friend helped me land a summer job with the State Road Department. After high school, I would work that summer as a crew member in a survey party. Armed with the seasonal job, a few dollars in the bank and a place to live near the campus, I looked forward to starting college in the fall. The money would be tight, but purpose and resolve drove me.

My enthusiasm rose as the final days of high school drew near that Spring of 1947. The end of the long fifteen-year term was at hand, so I paused to review my life.

The orphanage offered some things that few people had in 1932 — modern facilities. All the living quarters included electric lights, running water and indoor toilets. The buildings were steam heated. Grandfather's rustic farm in Knox County had none of these features, though our birthplace in Knoxville had all the comforts of a city house.

Though I was only four years old when we had to give it up, I recalled the happy home life we shared as a loving family. I greatly missed its warmth and security. After the move, the harsh realities of orphanage life dealt me a hard blow. It worsened when Mother left us there alone. My two sisters, brother and I formed a bond for our mutual comfort. This gave me the strength to live through the blues of those early years but I still missed Mother very much.

I continued the review of life at the orphanage, but skipped through the bad times and the painful business with Mr. Acree. I tried to look at the total picture — the good as well as the bad. In this regard, I saw the fifteen years spent there in a new light.

The bitter outlook of the early years had faded as the new bosses changed the way they ran the orphanage. The pressure eased when Mr. Acree left. Mr. Widgery's removal improved life to a lesser degree, as did Mr. Kilpatrick's exit a year or so later. I had spent a dozen trouble-filled years under these three superintendents. Finally, my life took a giant leap forward with Mr. Byrom's arrival.

A father-to-son kinship arose between us. Perhaps it was more grandfather to grandson, considering our ages. He seemed able to read my moods and proved in many ways that he cared for me as a person. This was a new experience. His warmth and style made the last three years at the orphanage bearable, if not crowned with pleasure.

Though it had been tough living through the bad times, I knew that the process had left me richer in many ways. I had gained a will to work, a good high school education and a set of sound moral values. These qualities would direct me to a fuller life.

> Life in the orphanage left me richer in many waysin spite of all the bad times. I gained a will to work, a good high school education and a set of sound moral values.

My life in the orphanage had favored me with many other strengths. I learned, while keeping my spirit intact, how to follow orders. I gained a healthy respect for authority and learned to work with others as a unit. I learned how to survive in a tough regimented system. The true value of these points would become clear later on, when I served in the Army.

Though I hated the idea of hard work, I learned how to grow a garden as well as many other tricks of farming. Because the times required it, I gained a good background in equipment repair. A trial and error process became my friend. The most important lessons I learned, however, were: "I am responsible for myself — no other will do my bidding. I, therefore, must carry my own weight."

That final day was near at hand at last, and I planned to leave the orphanage the following morning. At mid-afternoon, I found myself on an errand to the dairy barn. A sense of euphoria filled me when I thought about this last trip to the old hangout. After 15 long years, I was truly about to leave the orphanage. As I opened the barn door to walk out, a feeling of total freedom enveloped me. Immersed in this delightful new mood, I slipped into a state of total bliss.

The gravity of the moment stopped me in my tracks. I looked skyward. Billowy cotton clouds stretched across the blue sky. My mood and spirit soared as one with the view. The time is at hand; I'm leaving! I'm as free as the clouds!

Suddenly, a thought snapped into my head. I regressed ten years and was standing in the red clay field near the chicken house. Near this spot, I had accidentally cut down the tomato plant and Mr. Widgery had tried to expel me. This flash-back drew me to an earlier time, to a forgotten event that took place years earlier. It seems that I had programmed my brain to recall a certain matter on the day I was to leave the orphanage.

I was eight years old and with a group of boys I picking up the rocks embedded in the bright red dirt. An older boy heard me say that it hadn't been long since we gathered rocks from the same field. He said,

"These rocks really grow fast; That's why we need to pick them up so often, the little ones grow into big ones, you know."

I questioned,

"How is this possible? If true, how can I prove it?"

An idea popped into my head. I'd place a rock on a fence post and leave it there. On the day I was to leave the orphanage, I'd check to see if it had grown. Now, ten years later, my departure date was at hand and it was time to check the rock. I had used as a yardstick my last day at the orphanage — that seemed to be such a long time away.

When I snapped back from the ten-year time warp, my testing the boy's statement had lain dormant for years. I had kept faith with my memory. The entire fence had disappeared. We had removed it several years earlier, making it impossible to complete the test. Of course, now it wasn't necessary to check the growth of rocks.

I stood in the barnyard enjoying that spirit of perfect bliss. I wanted to engrave the scene into my memory as I'd done with the rock test. My entire being yielded to the feeling at hand — freedom at last. Surely, Thomas Jefferson had this sense of freedom in mind when he labeled it a gift from our Creator.

The Thrill of the Occasion Lives On.

I stood there submerged in the sight, sentiment and significance of that glorious day. The past, with its stress and trouble, had ended. The future, an open road filled with great promise, was now at hand. Responding to the passion of this moment, I wanted to embrace its magic forever. I looked up to the heavens. Several cotton-white clouds with gray linings marched across the brilliant blue sky and burned into my memory.

The thrill of the occasion still lives today. It returns each time I happen to see a like pattern of clouds — I bath in the splendor of that indescribable freedom.

END

BIBLIOGRAPHY and SOURCES

1. Personnel Records of the Tennessee Odd Fellows Home, in two volumes. These records, covering the 649 former residents who live there from 1899 to 1948, were under the supervision of Dr. Charles Worrell, Grand Secretary of the Independent Order of Odd Fellows (I.O.O.F.) Grand Lodge of Tennessee, 904 Gallatin Road, Nashville, Tennessee 32726.

2. *The History and Manual of Odd Fellowship,* by Theo. A. Ross, Past Grand Secretary of the Sovereign Grand Lodge, published 1911 in New York by the M. W. Hazen Company. (Mr. John Carney Sr. gave me this book, which Mr. Homer E. Neblett had owned and given him.).

3. Superintendent's Report to Board of Trustees, Odd Fellows Home of Tennessee, April 1, 1912, by T. M. Oakley, Supt. (Provided by Mr. Vester Powers.)

4. *Seventy-third Annual Session Proceedings of the Grand Lodge, I.O.O.F. of Tennessee,* Dated October 22, 1913. Report by Mr. E.E. York, Supt. of I.O.O.F. Home included. (Provided by Mr. Vester Powers).

5. *Odd Fellowship, What is it?* A six-page pamphlet written by Mr. J. R. Hartwell, Grand Secretary, Nashville, Tennessee dated December 21, 1903. This family heirloom is the very flyer that helped convince the author's maternal grandfather, James Marshall Dance, to join the Odd Fellows.

6. The *Tennessee Odd Fellow's* article entitled, "Odd Fellows Home," published in 1914. (Courtesy of Mr. Vester Powers.)

7. *Nineteenth Century Heritage (A History of Clarksville, Tennessee)* by Ursula S. Beach & Eleanor Williams Published by The Guild Bindery Press Oxford, Miss.

8. *Cemetery Records of Montgomery County, Volume 1,* Compiled by Anita Whitfield Darnell and others.

9. Extensive interviews with Mr. Vester Powers, former resident of the Home. Mr. Powers was head of the local Clarksville Odd Fellow Lodge during our several meetings.

10. Personal interviews with former residents Mr. John Carney Sr., Mr. Fleming Anderson, Mr. Oscar J. Lewis, and Mr. Ernest Johnson, during the summer of 1991.

11. Interview, on August 18, 1991, with Mrs. Frances Hambaugh Moore, former teacher at the orphanage. She taught the Author grades 1 through 7.

12. Interview, on April 13, 1992, with Mr. George Bridges, former resident of orphanage.

13. Interview with Mr. Sanders Anglea, former Grand Master of I.O.O.F. of Tennessee and former Grand Sovereign, I.O.O.F. of the United States. This took place on August 19, 1992, at his resident, 3701 Medowbrook Street, Nashville, Tennessee.

14. Telephone interview, during December 1992, with Woodroe W. Edwards, former resident of Odd Fellows Home.

15. Consultations with Ms. Edith Cook and Mr. Don Harris of Christ School in Arden, North Carolina on March 23, 1992.

16. Interview, on June 14, 1992, with Mr. Gilbert (Pete} Williams, the orphanage and director from 1933 to 1942.

17. During the early and mid 1990's, the author held many talks with people who attendaned the reunions of the former residents of the Odd Fellows Home. The association holds these annual meetings at the orphanage cemetery in Clarksville, Tennessee.

18. The Author held many discussions with his sisters, Mrs. June Dempsey and Mrs. Barbara Johnson and his brother, Mr. Fred Foster, all of who lived with him at the orphanage.